CRAZY USELESS CONCEPTS

and Breaking Through Them

Cindy M. White

Crazy Useless Concepts and Breaking Through Them

ISBN/SKU number 979-8-9915494-0-0

Published by **Game Shift Press** (GAMESHIFTPRESS.COM), SanLuis Obispo, California, January, 2025.

Manufactured in the United States of America

Disclaimer

Author, Cindy White, has studied spirituality, health, and healing for over 40 years, including research on the ideas expressed herein.

Some of her teachers are mentioned in the text and listed in Reading Suggestions at the end of the book. While this topic may be influenced by these teachers, similarities to any particular works are coincidental and unintended.

All content represents the author's own unique messages, opinions, beliefs, and personal experience. No part of this book was written by an AI (artificial intelligence) writing tool.

This book should not replace your current health care regimen. Seek a medical expert, therapist, and/or health practitioner when needed.

Sincere apologies if any phrase or viewpoint does not resonate with you, the reader. Please select and incorporate what serves you, and ignore the rest.

This book may change your life.

Dedicated to those seeking conscious travel,
and to our young impressionable generations ahead

May we all pave the way
for a concept-free
existence

Contents

INTRODUCTION

Only if you arrived on Earth yesterday would you notice the ridiculousness of the rules we live by. Have a good chuckle as you read our rules for eating potatoes.

You don't put mayonnaise on your home fries, but it's a main ingredient in potato salad. You would never put ketchup on your baked potato (yuck), but it's almost required for french fries. You wouldn't think of putting milk on your hash browns; however, you use it to make cream of potato soup. Who would ever dunk those fries into sour cream or a wad of butter? But those are standard toppings on a baked potato.

Are your eyes rolling? Don't forget about timing rules on when to eat potatoes! Those bakers are only for dinner, potato salad is for lunch, and hash browns are for breakfast, which is in the morning...but also after midnight, another acceptable time for eating breakfast.

You *know* I'm not kidding! We all live by every one of these arbitrary "potato rules." Just step outside the lines, and you'll get some raised eyebrows indeed for breaking the rules around crazy useless potato-eating concepts!

*   *   *

Last summer, I had an experience about concepts that left an impression on me. I walked out onto the balcony of my 5-star hotel room in Cozumel, Mexico, overlooking an expansive ocean view and a lush, landscaped pool where swim-up bars and lounge chairs were uniformly lined beside a large palapa. White sands finished this postcard-perfect view. As I gazed out, a greeting from my neighboring room broke my reverie.

Charlie, a friendly middle-aged man shared that he was from the small inland farming town of Tracy, California. I told him I was writing a book about concepts and shared my humorous rant on our crazy potato rules. He nodded, saying he fully agreed. He said that he had escaped from his hometown, and repeated the word "escaped" to point out that he meant what he said.

He then shared a favorite quote he made up that I treasure to this day.

"If you don't like who you are, then *become* who you truly want to *be*."

With that, he concluded, "Come along, dear." He took his beautiful, petite wife by the hand, and they drifted back into their hotel room and deliberately created dream life.

Charlie had a few things figured out. His quote sums up the main point of this book. However, to get there, we must clear away the formidable drift of invisible debris that stops us. I assert that this debris is unnecessary and self-imposed. It comprises a huge set of personally accepted constructs on how to live life that we unknowingly carry around. At some point, we went on "auto pilot" and didn't notice that many of our beliefs and behaviors hold us back in a myriad of ways. This book is an attempt to reveal this absurd trap I call *Crazy Useless Concepts*.

Though non-tangible, concepts are still very real. They have the same fortitude as a brick wall or an iron-bar cell keeping us from our best lives. These concepts undermine us, limit us, and whisper nay-saying putdowns. They act as a blanket to keep us safely small. They prevent us from trying new things and from walking down new roads in life. They spin us off balance and cause drama and ruined relationships. Many of our concepts tell more lies than truths. They bind us and blind us with irrelevant rules and invisible signposts. They dictate what we can and cannot do, and we don't even know this is happening.

Crazy Useless Concepts Illustrates this and invites us into conscious choice. While it pokes fun at our ridiculous human ways, on a deeper level it unwinds the knot we've gotten ourselves into and shines a light on the consequences and our escape route. The ultimate solution lies in spiritual awareness and acting on the insights that this awareness brings.

With a newfound awareness, we can form new ideas and expansive solutions for a brighter, healthier, and more successful life. This leads to greater personal freedom and a happier existence. Becoming concept-free, we become all we were meant to be.

We must open that door to better, more conducive choices to claim the freedoms we have never had. We can accomplish so many of our dreams! In short, dropping our concepts is life changing.

My great wish for you is to turn up the light on your life and consciously make your own decisions from a place of awareness, creativity, joy, and self-love.

*   *   *

Let's face it: Life does not come with a manual. We don't know what we're doing most of the time, nor why. Oh sure, we can come up with a great reply, "I go to work, raise my children, pay the bills, and seek happiness and fulfillment." But do you? Were all these your choices? Are you really navigating life deliberately, or are you playing out someone else's script unknowingly?

Do we have clarity on the deepest level? Do we really know who or what creates everything, what stars are, or even how electricity works? Do we know who *we* really are? If you answer, "I'm not exactly sure" to these questions, you're wise. Wise ones acknowledge all they don't know, and purposely live with a cup half empty to leave space for the ever expanding new.

If you appreciate the model of the half-full cup, you have space to learn. If your cup is full of, "I'm right" or "I'm just fine, thanks," you may have a good life, but tend to resist new ideas. Allow yourself the possibility to adopt the creative insights this book offers so your life can be even more amazing.

Who would you be if you weren't stuck with the concepts and behaviors that no longer work for you? Who would you be if you stepped out of your routine and chose a different life? Reducing ourselves to the goal of collecting stuff, checking items off our to-do lists, and enjoying entertainment may not be enough to bring us into our best lives.

Just for now, put your plans, lists, and schedules on pause. Living from a plan allows no space for spontaneity or freedom to take advantage of novel opportunities. Take the risk to live each day in the present moment. Set aside time to experience the *divine right now,* and watch what happens as you grow your ability to just *be.* In this simple profound moment, embrace the astonishing light and love that you are!

*   *   *

When this book uses humor and storytelling, it is not to ridicule or put down, but to challenge the ingrained concepts that have led to mundane and senseless behaviors. This book emphatically points out our crazy blind spots and limiting comfort zones hoping for a chuckle prior to redirecting ourselves. Humor can help us stop taking life so seriously and lift us to a place where we can snap out of our hardened, mental focus. Once you become aware of your own pitfalls and land mines, you are on your way to grabbing the wheel of your life and steering it appropriately.

The biggest goal of this book is to help you live an incredible, expansive life of your own choosing, free of debilitating concepts. We do this by harnessing the ability to notice and break our self-defeating patterns as they arise. With this new skill, we become free to live true to our Soul's path. We are then aligned with our talents and passions. We are empowered and free.

When changing anything, it's natural to feel fear. We may even feel unworthy or guilty, like a kid in the kitchen reaching for the cookie jar when no one is watching. You know the feeling, "Dare I go there just because I want to?"

I say, "Take that cookie. It's gluten-free, sugar-free, and packed with all the ingredients for a thriving, unique, and amazing life!" Take the challenge to become true to your deeper self.

On this path, don't worry about getting it right, or looking good. As humans, we are not perfect, nor should perfection be our goal; rather, our goal is to take the next step with loving self-acceptance, imperfections and all. In other words, our goal is to become self-aware, authentic, and empowered.

Dare to let yourself be real, alive, messy, emotional, and unskilled. When we stop criticizing and stifling ourselves, worrying, and trying to be like everyone else, we can relax into self-acceptance. Without inner conflict, we become present to the voice of our higher calling and can respond freely and powerfully.

This pull toward a freer, more authentic life is a calling, a higher calling. This is your chance to break through the patterns and concepts that have kept you sleepwalking through your life.

As you read on, I encourage you to embark on this new journey of discovery and hope. I promise that a heart-centered adventure awaits!

1 Exactly What Are Concepts?

I like to read dictionary definitions, including the Old English version to find out where our words and their suffixes and prefixes come from. Then I'll look up a word from the definition taking me on a Webster's magical mystery tour for more clarity. Here's what I found about the word *concept*.

Dictionary.com's definition of *concept*

con·cept

Noun

1. A general notion or idea; conception.
2. An idea, a construct.
3. A directly intuited object of thought.
4. Something conceived in the mind.
5. An abstract or generic idea generalized from a particular instance.

Word Origin & History

Origin: 1550–1560; < Latin conceptum: something conceived.

concept

History: 1550s, from M. L. conceptum "draft, abstract," concipere "to take in" (see conceive).

In some 16th century cases, a refashioning of conceit (perhaps to avoid negative connotations).

Hmmm, that's interesting. What is the definition of conceit?

Dictionary.com's definition of conceit

noun

1. An excessively favorable opinion of one's own ability, importance, wit.
2. Something conceived in the mind; a thought; idea.
3. Imagination; fancy.
4. A fancy; whim; fanciful notion.
5. An elaborate, fanciful metaphor, especially of a strained or far-fetched nature.

From all this, I gathered that a concept, whether intuited or analyzed, is something that we create in our own minds. Nowhere did I see the word "fact" or "truth" in these definitions. Concept's origin, "conceit," says that concepts can be fanciful, whimsical, and far-fetched. Therefore, we don't want to confuse "Truth" with "Concepts," and flood our lives full of far-fetched notions.

That being said, not all concepts are problematic. Concepts we formulate can serve us in many ways. They are our personal grasp of reality. Concepts are the mental building blocks that, when formulated, create great things: businesses, bridges, masterpieces, and inventions.

This book only refers to the *faulty concepts* we unknowingly adopt and live by, which cause us harm. I define these harmful "Crazy Useless Concepts" in this way:

A faulty set of beliefs formulated from faulty interpretations of life that prompt faulty strategies to manage the struggles in life.

* * *

If you decide to go fishing for your daily meal, you're innovative! But if you sit in one spot on a dock, using gear you've never learned how to use, and you've never seen or caught a fish before, you may have a relaxing time. However, as for catching a fish, you're probably out of luck as you are stuck in a faulty concept of how to fish.

This is because you aren't interfacing with the world or asking for the help you need. You aren't looking into the many lakes and rivers in your area. You are repeating an action without reassessing the results. You stopped thinking and became snagged in a closed loop hoping for something new: catching a fish.

This example seems too obvious, but it is exactly how we function in our daily lives. We don't always reassess or seek professional help and advice. We don't try new things every day or go to places we've never been. We don't take many risks, and we don't always put in the extra effort needed. Yet we want that fish! We want a happy, expansive life.

A crazy concept is a fixed state superimposed on an ever-changing world. On a personal level, it's a mindless way of being that eliminates all your many opportunities.

I want you to get so annoyed by the ruinous nature of concepts that you break through yours, slough them off like sweaty workout clothes, and finally remove them from the wide-open possibility of your life!

Imagine that you are the sleeping giant in *Gulliver's Travels* who awakens to find a sinister web of tiny threads restraining you. You're capable of grabbing these light strands and tossing them off with ease. But you can't, because you're asleep. So, you don't.

We must wake up to notice that the concepts we live by have wrapped us in a cocoon of limitation. We're like that giant, held down by mere threads of faulty belief systems, negative ideas, and silly fears. Until we recognize what we are doing to ourselves, we remain ensnared by the restraints we've placed in our mind.

2   Embracing Change

So, if this now makes sense, that breaking through our limiting concepts, our unserving thoughts and behavior patterns, is more advantageous than maintaining them, why wouldn't we just change? Perhaps it is because we don't want to do the work or face any fears. Making these changes also requires effort. It involves cognitive reassessments and action steps. It requires stepping into the unknown, and we simply don't want to go there.

Unknowns are scary for many people, yet the results we want come *after* this work. Perhaps, we are too busy or too exhausted at the end of the day to do much more than watch TV, eat, throw back a couple drinks, and go to bed. So, shunning all this effort, we opt for the easy path of doing what we always do, saying what we always say, and living in a similar, boring daily loop.

Change requires critical thinking. To begin something new, like learning a foreign language or even walking down a different street, takes greater brain function. You must look at new information and assess it against what you already know. You'll need to do calculations. "If I drive a different route to work, will I be late? How many traffic lights are there, driving that way? How many minutes will all those red lights slow me down?"

Change brings a host of new factors to consider, which can feel more unsettling than repeating what we know. In a larger context than your daily commute, when planning a travel adventure, you might want to ask, "Will I be safe traveling in this foreign country?" Answering that question will require some research. Without considering the overwhelming benefits that change offers, we are too often apt to choose the path of least effort, which is sameness and smallness.

However, change is inevitable; it happens whether we flow with or resist it. Change can meet us unprepared. We receive a Notice to Vacate. Or, we drop the ball on an event because we're "too nervous about it." We think we're protecting ourselves by procrastinating. In many cases, it's better to ride that uncertain wave of change than miss life's best opportunities.

Where will this wave of change lead us? The unknown can cause enough stress that we decide not to change. The layers of mental resistance are why people fall into grooves, continuing the same behaviors in life that make for a seemingly safe yet less than dynamic existence.

Here's a little secret: taking a new path requires more energy only at the *beginning*! You've got to push through inertia. Think of it as priming a pump; you'll need to repeatedly pump the handle, before water starts flowing from the well. Similarly, making cognitive and behavioral changes, seeking information, and taking action is like priming your pump. Doing these things forms a new synapse in the brain. *Repeating* these new behaviors carves deeper grooves in the brain's neural pathways. The more you repeat something new, the easier it becomes.

Before long, *choosing* the new behavior is effortless. The skill to stay the course becomes way more fluid and routine. You have created *momentum*.

We *can* change! We can "be the change we want to see in the world" as eloquently expressed and exemplified by the great political leader, Mahatma Gandhi. We can achieve the many things we set our minds to. We have the great gift of free will. When we practice these principles and hone these new skills, we will become our own great master in our life.

*   *   *

This brings us to the topic of insincere or inappropriate change. This refers to changing in the name of being hard on or forcing ourselves to do something we might not be ready for.

If we will just ask within, in each moment, what to do, where to go, what to say, and what is most important, this will provide a sincere path of choosing the next best right thing.

You can receive all the guidance you need from your gut (also known as intuition, common sense, or Spirit, God, Source. Use whatever orientation feels right for you). Proceeding according to your inner wisdom ensures you make the best choices for yourself and for everyone around you. It ensures that you are living concept-free.

You may be a list maker. Writing to-do lists is a great way to manage a detailed life. Apply a time frame to each item and distinguish your "must-dos" from the "would-be-nice-to-dos." If a to-do item lingers on your list for too long, cross it off the list in peaceful resolve. This is how you release inappropriate change.

Many things we want to do are based on concepts of what we *think* we must do. We learn or inherit much of our world picture from others. We must continuously ask if what we're doing is true to our life path, and is for our highest good. People pleasing and herd mentality will pull you away from your true heart's path. The word "should" signals that you may be urging yourself to do something insincere.

This is not to say it's Ok to break agreements with others. In every instance, keep your word. Find, with grace, your alignment between thought and speech and action while doing the least harm to others. It's also not wise to quit when the going gets tough. Once you embark on a true goal, do it with your whole heart and mind and body.

Eventually, every line item, appointment, errand, job, phone call, and project on your list will bring you joy, even gratitude, as you pay your bills, clean your house, and tend your garden. A shift in attitude to appreciation is the final formula that will release resistance and make your life meaningful.

*   *   *

At this point, I hope you are considering letting go of some unpleasant *should*s on your to-do list, items you've probably been grappling with for a while. While it may contain some anxiety, this change is not dangerous.

For example, declining a party invitation when you really don't want to go might cause a bit of disappointment among other attendees, but you can offer to meet someone another time. Taking this mild risk after listening to your intuition will allow you to take care of yourself and find creative solutions to support others, while staying in your truth. This is a win-win! You get to learn that every concept you release, in this case not attending an event that you clearly are not feeling right about, teaches that you can stay loving, and stay in your truth, and stay on your path.

Becoming more engaged in your life is about living in balance with certainty and change. The reward of mastering this is more confidence, more wisdom, and more ease and fluidity around your next steps. Keep changing your mind and making concept-free life decisions until you arrive in your best life. Ask your Self for the ideas, insights, and most appropriate information for the moment. You may be surprised that you can hear your inner voice and even dialog with it.

There's only one you, and there are only so many hours in the day. You're an amazing person! You know how to live without that drill sergeant in your ear. We pile extra unpleasant baggage on our loads and wonder why we're so tired. With the time you'll gain from not over-scheduling or living from a plan, you get to breathe into lightness. By not filling your days with unnecessary *shoulds*, you gain hours of peace. This one idea, leaving a bit of free time for yourself each day, reduces stress and overwhelm from not being able to pursue personal rewards. We could use this extra time to brainstorm a new dream or two or do nothing at all to unwind from life.

Emptying our mental bucket, reducing our schedule, and scrubbing the *shoulds* from our lives leaves more space for the diversity and magic of life to show up. What's possible is more clarity and creativity. So, play around with allowing open, non-scheduled time for this type of change.

An ongoing to-do list is essential for accomplishing more in an organized and efficient way, but a pared down to-do list is essential to living a Soul-guided life. When you leave open amounts of time in your day, Spirit trickles in. Stay present to the gifts that are *already* in your daily life. Rushing can make you pass them by. Be proud of your favorite, ever-changing, life. It's really all a miracle.

Thank you for summoning the courage to become aligned with your True Self; this kind of change changes everything. Thank you for rising to the occasion of staying present in each new moment and choosing what's right for you in loving compassion. Fear of change, in comparison, is an empty concept with a false promise of safety it can never deliver. The most you risk by stepping through your fears to making wonderful changes in your life is that nothing works out. But then, you will have tried. You will collect some life experiences and more knowledge. You will ace it on your next attempt! It's always worth it to try your best because *you* are worth it! And if there's some rough edges around finding that true path, remember this favorite Zen saying:

"Fall down seven times, get up eight."

Making concept-free life choices in every moment is cooperating with the intelligence of the Divine. You begin to source a deeper wisdom when you stay in tune with yourself instead of clinging to concepts, fears, or your prearranged plan. When you quiet yourself by meditating or taking a walk in nature, you can begin to hear the wisdom of your Higher Self. This is living on your true path to success!

3   Quick Defeatist Conclusions

Concepts are present when we have all these arbitrary and unnecessary rules around how to do things in life, such as in the example of how to eat potatoes. Here's a miserable, yet all too familiar, scene about being stuck in a concept with no possibility of a solution.

Shirley is an attractive 38-year-old getting ready for her 20th high school reunion. She heads into her large walk-in closet, grabs item after item off the hangers, and tosses them on the floor. Within five minutes she declares, "I have *nothing* to wear!"

Shirley's neatly organized closet houses over eighty pairs of shoes—fifty are heeled, twenty are flat, five are for hiking, and five are slippers. She has eighty tops. Some are short-sleeved, some are long-sleeved or sleeveless, some are blousy, and the rest are casual tee shirts. Shirley has thirty-five pairs of pants, three-dozen dresses, ten skirts, four gauchos, and two business suits. But at that moment, she had *nothing* to wear!

Shirley works herself up into a frenzy as she becomes late for her event. She isn't dressed, and she hasn't done her makeup or her hair. Sweat forms in her pits and glistens on her forehead. Rushing to the bathroom, she trips over a mountain of clothes, twists her ankle, and breaks a nail.

Are you relating? Has this ever been you or your partner? Shirley created an enormously stressful situation, making herself totally frustrated, helpless, and late for her event. She teetered on canceling her long-awaited big night because of her quick defeatist conclusions! She was mired down by the stranglehold of nothing but a concept.

This scene is all too common. It's a woman's worst nightmare. Have you ever wondered where this craziness comes from? Shirley doesn't lack intelligence, so how does she equate a full walk-in closet with "nothing to wear?"

Here's a possibility: Shirley isn't just looking at her clothes. She's attached history and emotions to them. She is looking at her past judgments and criticisms, her earlier, less mature years, and all the disappointments she had while wearing those clothes. She isn't in the present moment. She isn't seeing clearly. Shirley is snagged in a web of crazy concepts that she unconsciously attached to her clothing.

No one complimented that blouse. Those pants made her look fat. That dress isn't in fashion anymore. (Never mind that "in fashion" no longer matters—none of this is logical).

Shirley wore that black top on the sad day she and Alvin broke up. She couldn't throw it away, but knew she would never wear it again. Shirley wore this business suit, but didn't get the job. Someone laughed at that pair of shoes, but they were too expensive to throw away. She'd heard somewhere that "white is out," so she won't wear anything white. Yet, it all hangs in her closet, clean and perfectly fine, except for the judgments woven into the fabric. All these unwearable clothes reminded her of all the past situations that didn't go so well. Her closet no longer contained a wardrobe; it was a land mine of bad memories and loaded concepts!

Old memory-based concepts are nasty possibility thieves. They irrationally dictate what's Ok and what's not Ok. If someone walking into a massive closet believes she has "nothing to wear," this type of concept wipes out 99% of our legitimate choices. Clinging to these concepts from the past steals our peace of mind and common sense. In this example, it ended up stealing her positive attitude, time with favorite childhood connections, and a fingernail.

When feverishly searching and becoming increasingly stressed, accidents happen. Rushing through life can cause you to stub your toe or drive over the speed limit. If you rush through assignments at work or school, you make errors or cut corners when details are required; you miss things. Your patience leaks away; you yell at your kids and argue with your partner. People in a rush are frequently impatient, overwhelmed, and angry.

An arbitrary stranglehold is in charge. An ominous, invisible judge is directing this show. The judge finally allows Shirley to choose an outfit, but she is full of doubt and angst as she rushes out the door late to her event.

*   *   *

Let's put on our thinking caps. Does anyone really care which outfit we wear, as long as it's modestly appropriate to the venue? Did the clothing choice for this event warrant that much drama? People don't want to see your perfect outfit; they want to see *you*. Actually, they just want to see you happy.

So, when searching for your next outfit, recall Shirley's whirlwind scene and catch yourself mid-flight. Do you care what other people wear, despite the invitation prompt? Will you think badly if someone comes too formally dressed or in a more casual outfit than requested? Now, do you think—or care—that anyone will have a second thought about what you wear? Do you think anyone will remember your outfit the next day? You can use these questions if you find yourself stuck in this type of concept, a quick defeatist conclusion where you imagine there is *no possible solution to the situation,* and it's impossible to select an acceptable outfit.

Similar defeatist conclusions include the ever-popular, "I'm bored, *there's nothing to do.*" Or *"There's nothing to eat in this house."* Quick defeatist conclusions can also be snap judgments on our abilities. Examples of this include

"I can't draw; I'm not an artist."

"I'm not good at math, writing, spelling, foreign languages, remembering names, sports, cooking, or fixing things, etc."

If you take classes and continue studying and practicing, you will eventually become great at these skills! You can learn unlimited amounts of talents, tasks, and hobbies by watching YouTube instructional videos. There is a wealth of information online, ample adult education classes, workshops, and books you can check out from the library. Many of these educational tools are free of charge.

There are many ways to learn anything you want to learn. Therefore, refrain from deciding you can't do something, you don't know how, or worse, you *aren't good at something* when you haven't taken the time to learn and practice it. Look to see if you've attached a sad moment in the past to the skill, and you are suffering from the memory of a past traumatic moment.

Like the stranglehold we have on our clothes, we associate bad memories with activities. We may have decided we aren't interested in sports, but in truth, we fell off our go-cart when we were nine and skinned our knees. The experience was extremely scary! Or we were booed off the stage after singing in a talent show in high school. Mortified from this experience, we became an introvert and decided we *can't sing*.

From a place of trauma, we generalize. We also decide to never try whatever-it-was again, based on one clueless teacher's comment. We refused to ever speak publicly. We even decided we hate crowds. None of these decisions were conscious. They became protective mechanisms and remained in place. Making decisions from a place of trauma results in a myriad of quick defeatist conclusions. The brain signals us to avoid all situations like this. Years later, you continue to believe you cannot do something or don't like it, and forget the real reason why.

Our brains have a predisposition for left-side or right-side dominance. The right-brain dominant person will prefer artistry, language, and aesthetics such as design, literature, painting, and cooking. Left-brain dominant persons will have more ease with analytical topics such as math, architecture, and the sciences. But your brain dominance or even your IQ doesn't preclude you from learning any topic in life! Many don't realize this when they say, "I'm left-brained; therefore, I don't have any artistic talent."

It's debilitating when we mistake our tendencies for the totality of possible talents we can have, and never attempt to learn in less comfortable areas. Further, thinking in black and white terms, "I'm good at this, but not at that," prevents the possibility of becoming better at what we aren't so good at now.

You might think, "It's not my thing." What does this mean? Ask yourself, "Where did that quick, defeatist statement come from?" Inquiry at this juncture may reveal a block you can easily release. Dropping limiting beliefs around our abilities can return energy to us. More importantly, it returns curiosity and the excitement to try new things.

Never questioning our concepts solidifies our notions and creates walls around our thinking and routine. No one is making life hard on us. We think the thoughts that stop us; and these thoughts turn our options to cement.

Then we believe, "That's just the way it is." "That's the way the cookie crumbles." "That's life." All these sayings are declarations of quick defeatist conclusions. They aren't true or real; they are only concepts.

Solving this grim situation is what this book is about. We choose to melt the concepts that keep us stuck in no possibility. We awaken to the truth that fixed states of defeat are unnecessary, and that it's never too late to learn something. Life constantly requires us to keep growing, and this includes learning new skills. Therefore, our success in life must include a continual process of education. By the way, when we say, "Yes" to learning, it becomes fun!

If you ever find yourself in the mental quicksand of "I can't," stop and ask yourself, "Am I thinking clearly? Is this true? Do I really have nothing to wear, nothing to eat, nothing to do, or no talent? Are my snap judgments serving me? Does it really matter what I put on today? Can I wear something I don't usually wear? Can I change my mind about what is attractive or looks cool? Can I reveal another dimension of myself by wearing certain clothes? Can I dress artsy, sporty, retro, country, or Renaissance today?"

When you consider this line of inquiry, you give yourself a new direction and lease on life. You open a rich opportunity to know how this universe ticks. You give yourself the reward of achievement. You start knowing yourself as unstoppable. You begin seeing all the stoplights turn green.

Breaking free from defeatist language naturally allows you to live in greater possibility. This allows for sane and practical thinking. It helps your brain function better when you remove the quick defeatist brakes. You'll be on your way to plentiful choices that were formerly out of reach. Once you sharpen this skill, you will no longer need to protect yourself with quick defeatist conclusions; you'll replace them with "I can," "I will be able to," and "I'm not sure, but I can find out."

The next time you find yourself saying, "I can't spell, fix things, make a lot of money, or find love," interrupt yourself and say:

"Wait, this is not true; it's only a concept! Did I have a bad experience in this area? Oh yes, I remember that time in 5th grade. Now, do I want to overcome this block and learn this now?"

Likely, the older, wiser version of you is more capable than you were when you couldn't do it. Another truth may be that you aren't good at something because you have no interest in the subject. We don't have to be great at everything. We don't have to do it all. We can delegate the skills and tasks we do not want to learn to accountants, contractors, and marketing specialists.

It could be that you *are* pretty good at the subject at hand, but you aren't giving yourself enough credit. Our low self-impressions are covered more fully in another chapter.

The best redirect when you catch yourself in a self-limiting concept is to add the term, *yet*. "I haven't mastered this *yet.*" When you add this little word to your lack of success statement, your brain prepares for accomplishing and becoming good at this in the future. In short, "yet" holds open the door to possibility. It implies, "I'm becoming a good artist," or "I will be great at knitting." Or "I'm not a New York Times best-selling author *yet.* (But I can be)."

Another trick to moving defeatist statements into possibility is to refer to failure as having happened in the past. For example: "I wasn't good at remembering names, but now I have fun repeating the name three times during a conversation when I meet someone, and I associate their name with an image that helps me remember their name."

This is how you do it! Your brain then starts to look for *when* you will do it, *what it takes* to do it, and *how* you will accomplish this new activity.

Catching quick defeatist conclusions and asking the right questions can launch you into skill development. Ask, "What does it take to master this situation, skill, or ability?" "What skills do I need to get this job?" "How can I learn how to do my own handyman work so I can save money?"

The answers to these questions will become clear when you let go of those quick defeatist conclusions and allow yourself to consider all your options.

Learning and improving do not always require formal education. Sometimes, solving a problem means letting go of it, just like you'd let go of a hot pot you unknowingly grabbed. This example requires no education, no thought process, and no time to develop any skills! In life, we occasionally have to drop a hot pot. So, call out, "Hot pot!" and drop those things that don't serve you like it's burning your hand! It's really that easy to drop bad habits once you decide they are hot pots.

Other times our crazy concepts take more digging. For example, to dispel "I have nothing to wear," you could ask, "What made me get so uptight that night?" The answers will reveal your concepts. From there, you can form great solutions.

Use this issue-solution method on any quick defeatist statement you engage in.

1) Catch yourself when you are stuck in a concept.

2) Declare that the concept you are believing is not true.

3) Write the details of the issue, the mood, the struggle, the faulty belief. After the issue,

4) Write a solution that feels right to you.

5) Get a notebook and keep an ongoing log of these. It's a powerful tool to rewrite your concepts, and get to reread them to reinforce your new solutions.

If you train your mind to do this with every defeatist concept, small and large, you'll quickly pop out of the spiral of defeat and be on the hunt for creative solutions.

Become a lifelong self-learner. The quick defeatist gives up too early on themselves. Your personal power, self-trust, and peace of mind are priceless commodities. These are the just a few of the many gifts that you'll embody once you master this concept.

4   Silly Slavery Mentality

"I must go to work full time at a low-paying job that I can barely tolerate, where there is too much stress, people I don't get along with, and no opportunity to use my greatest talents or passions. I'll struggle through 45 minutes of rush-hour traffic, take my two weeks' vacation each year, and, after several years, I'll get a raise. I'll start at the bottom and work my way up the ladder; then I'll be a success." Hmmm. Might you be stuck in a slavery mentality?

"I must remain in a relationship where I'm unhappy, live in a place where I don't feel comfortable, buy products I don't need, watch the news, and carry the burden of life." No, you don't. In fact, *please don't*. No one has to endure the stress, sadness, smallness, and half-hearted efforts to succeed in an insincere life.

You may not even realize you're doing this to yourself. You may be mistaking these things that are weighing you down for being responsible or doing what's expected. You may have no idea how much priceless joy and energy you're missing out on by trudging a dead-end career path. This chapter offers the gift of reassessing a few things, and challenges you to cut the inauthenticity out of your life, here and now—for good.

This self-defeating concept is sad. The only reason I use the term "silly" in the title is to bring lightness to a grave situation, hoping if we decide that living this way is silly, we'll snap out of it.

Who decided that survival requires endless toil for little remuneration or reward of any kind? Nothing could be further from the case of your endless possibilities.

Have you ever noticed that wait staff in the most expensive restaurants do the least amount of work? They make gentle conversation, take the orders, and deliver the beautifully plated food. At the end of the meal, they quietly set down the check and receive praise for a job well done.

Bus staff on the other hand, do the bulk of the work. They prep the table, and bring the silverware, soup, salad, and water. They return to remove dirty dishes after each course, then prepare the table for the next party. Fine dining servers earn three to four times more than bus staff for a fraction of the work.

Flash frame to a coffee shop. Servers work fast and hard. They perform all the serving duties: taking the order, filling the soup and salad bowls, bringing each course. They bus and set their own tables. They make repeated trips to top off the water. After all the hustle and effort, it's not uncommon to receive a modest tip or even a refused tip if something wasn't just right, like an unfilled coffee cup. Why is this?

It is *quality*, not quantity, that makes something valuable. Quality is timeless. It is a feeling, a pace, and an intention to deliver an exquisite *experience*.

We may think that value is in quantity, but that's not usually the case. Value is a subjective and intangible experience of quality that only the heart recognizes. Quality is not getting more and paying less; it comes from feelings of satisfaction and gratitude. Value comes from *increased appreciation* for someone or something, and by experiencing a person or situation to be rare, special, priceless, and lovely.

Quality, being out of the time-space continuum, is effortless. Attempting to attain value by spending the least money, effort, and appreciation yields less value not more.

So work smart, not hard. Aim for a quality life, not just a number of work hours. It is appreciation, perspective and experience that leads to quality, not unsatisfying hard work with little pay.

Sure, living any kind of life takes effort and energy. But when you are involved with people and situations that are in high integrity and who exude gratitude, your life can become far richer with far less effort. When you seek a profession that aligns with your Higher Will vs. your ego, your joy and your God-given talents will flow effortlessly. It's like surfing a wave crest—exhilarating and fun! Think of work as getting to do what you love most and what you are best at. Focus on the enjoyment rather than effort. Live in this place rather than in have-to toil and drudgery.

Celebrate this truth: If higher paying jobs are physically less challenging, and providing quality work enhances value in your life, your work doesn't have to be a struggle for you! Regardless of your level of employment and income, a persistent feeling of struggle could be a sign that you're trying too hard, not in the right job, or swimming against the current in some way. Bring inquiry into your career and use your journal to write down your issues around work. Then formulate solutions including action steps and changes in thinking.

Before resigning, clear all your issues within yourself. You may find a solution that restores balance and all you value about your position.

Are you interested in a no-struggle life? Then affirm it. Speak this out loud:

"I am a quality being extending quality work. I live an abundant exquisite life! I appreciate myself and others, and good comes to me all the time. I am in the flow of life with a heart overflowing in gratitude for what I have and who I am. I give thanks that this is so. So be it, and so it is!"

Remember, value comes from the quality of our thoughts (concepts) and our presence, not the quantity of money, the prestige, or the stuff. High quality and value derive from accepting that *life already is this valuable* then dropping into the appreciation of this truth.

Quality does not wait for some point in the future, and it cannot be manufactured or bought. *Quality is a perspective that we accept as true NOW.*

Let these truths heal you from the painful efforts you've endured in your life and from the joy you believe you've missed out on. It's not possible to live in the future, so refrain from the idea that once X, Y, or Z happens (such as when I find my true love, when the kids go off to college, or when I retire), I'll be happy. I'll have arrived at success. Attaching your happiness to the outside world is a losing struggle. Choose happiness and deep contentment now. As Marcy Shimoff[1] says, "Be happy for no reason." Choose self-love. Living with an open heart and mind leads to a high quality, exquisite life. It magnetizes it.

Purge the crazy concept called, "I *have* to." Be thoroughly convinced that effort doesn't always create success, nor does lots of money create happiness. In fact, happiness and satisfaction are inner achievements felt from following and completing your own definitions of success.

Value is how we appreciate, not what we get. Let go of silly slave mentality, such as *"things take a long time,"* or that

---

[1] Marci Shimoff & Carol Kline, *Happy for No Reason: 7 Steps to Being Happy from the Inside Out,* 2008. Free Press.

you must work long hours for your bread and butter. Be relieved to know that this is not the formula for success; the formula is much easier and relies on your willingness and ability to question, "What do I love to do?" and "What higher paying jobs entail the least amount of stress, have fewer hours and earn a lot of money?" You could Google this question and receive a hundred jobs that fit this description.

Discard your crazy concepts about earning a living. If you want to learn more about the inner mindset and lifestyles that create wealth, read *The Millionaire Next Door* by Thomas J. Stanley, and *Rich Dad, Poor Dad* by Robert Kiyosaki. For an understanding of the flow and magnetism of energy, read *Creating Money; Keys to Abundance* by Sanaya Roman and Dwayne Packer. More is said in chapter 10; Concepts around Money.

"Who says?" is a good question to ask yourself when you catch yourself suffering around the requirement to do anything. You are hereby given permission to rewrite your truth around silly slavery mentality!

Declare the following:

- I can have the life I want. Things come easy for me.
- Everything serves my highest good.
- My success comes to me instantly and perfectly.

- I claim an easy, joy-filled, and abundant life.

- I need not struggle to get my needs met.

- I enjoy ample free time.

- I break my pact with hark work for little pay. I am free of silly slavery mentality!

- My vocation serves me and everyone around me. I am truly blessed.

- I love my life. All is well.

5   Believing Your Past Defines You

This crazy concept speaks to those who believe they are defined by their genetics, past experiences, ancestry, gender, skin color, and the inextricable stereotypes that swarm around these and other factors, like religion, education, and social and economic standing. This concept assumes that a certain background or personal history dictates that you and your life are locked into a certain definition.

This crazy concept convinces you that your past follows you into your present and will always determine your future. You are who you are because of the past. You have no say in the matter. You're shaped, you're gifted, judged, or permanently screwed because of what happened one day, back then.

However, the past and this moment are unrelated. This moment is connected to an all-potent presence. The now is all there is. The past no longer exists; it is only a memory, which tends to change and fade over time. The time is always now. Basing our identity on the past is truly crazy thinking.

This is not to say that our past experiences were not truly valuable or impactful. But once we begin to see that we are no longer the same being we once were, regardless of the circumstances, we get to change.

When we release identification with our past, we get to have an entirely free present. We can have and embrace a life filled with reality and ample possibility. Tomorrow isn't a continuation of yesterday unless you make it one. Yesterday is an impression of reality that we form in our own minds.

Do not confuse reality with a thought. This mistake brings you to believe that the past dictates your identity. You become only the formulations of what happened in the past. You aren't in the present moment anymore—you are past referenced, snared in a concept.

Mentally dwelling in the past (such as regret) and in the future (such as worry) allows our thoughts to control us. These tendencies keep us in our heads instead of living from our hearts. Believing we are the story of our past traps our identity in a story. Believing in some future doom hinders us from freely moving forward. We can redirect ourselves to stay more in the present so these crazy lost-in-time concepts don't trap us indefinitely.

*   *   *

If you hit another car on the road, do you say, "I'll never drive again?" If you have a disappointing relationship, do you swear off ever meeting anyone else? "Of course not," you say, "these are silly questions."

But many of us end up avoiding an entire area of life because of one bad experience in our past. This is a quick defeatist conclusion. It's also a problem of being past referenced, and how we think, subconsciously, when we're protecting ourselves. "Once burned, twice shy" (as the saying goes) leads us into a fear-based decision to never do *that* again.

We generalize that this particular event is true for every similar situation and then shut down out of fear that the same bad experience will happen again. This is how we allow the past to rule our futures. Interestingly, there's no universal law that says if you fail or hurt yourself, you are likely to repeat the same harm again. Rather, the chances of that same thing happening are *less* likely because we've hopefully learned from the experience.

The past can serve and teach us; it doesn't have to scare us or shut us down. When we allow ourselves to learn from past experiences, we collect and integrate important information and use it to serve our next steps.

This is not to say that painful experiences, no matter how distant in the past, are easy to release. If you were sexually assaulted, injured in a bad car accident, or diagnosed with a life-threatening illness, no one would deny the severity of these experiences. You are a survivor. But, when you're ready, ask yourself how to stop being a survivor and start becoming a thriver in spite of all you've been through.

Another trap of referencing ourselves to the past is when we confuse our identity with our level of education and school we graduated from and let this become our identity. It is nice to have an MA or a PhD after our name. Many authors, scholars, and professionals lean heavily on their academic background for clout by using their credentials to get their messages across. It helps to get jobs and exhibits their level of dedication. The problem arises when our ego uses it to bolster our self-worth. This creates problems if we think we are better than those without an education, and we misplace where our real power lies.

Our identity and worth always lie within, not in reference to a past action. Our worth cannot be defined by anything we did or didn't do in the outer world. Your worth is YOU in this present moment, because *you exist as a profound beautiful being*. Nothing else is required. Nothing else can replace your existence as the apex of your worth. You are 100% completely worthy now, without any need to provide reasons, accomplishments, or proof. Take a breath into this truth of your true worth. Let go of all the albeit nice, but false reasons for your worth. This is a very different statement that brings the power back into you.

As you begin to let go of your concepts around identifying with a sad, proud, happy, or empty past, these events have one thing in common—they are over. They all can help you, but they don't define you.

Identity is a concept: I'm a veteran, I'm agnostic, I'm a female. These are careers and beliefs and genders. They are wonderful but needn't be confused with who you really are. Notice the difference in the truth and power within the following true identity statements:

- I am awareness. I am pure divine Love. I am Presence.

- I am made in the image and likeness of God. I am made of Light. I am at Peace.

- I am one with my Source, the source of all that is. I am beautiful, whole, and complete.

Just to be is a blessing. Just to live is Holy.

Abraham Joshua Hershel

---

6 TORTURING OURSELVES WITH CONCEPTS

You might be thinking, "I don't torture myself."

But how critical are you of yourself? How often and for how long do you berate and belittle yourself for your perceived infractions? Do you compare yourself to others and notice all the ways you fall short? This is torture!

We flog ourselves in so many ways for so many imagined failings. We believe crazy concepts about how we're supposed to be and then berate ourselves when we fall short of our self-defined ideals. We don't make the mark in our own minds. We don't say the right things. We forget to do something, so we punish ourselves. We can scold ourselves endlessly for the same mistake we've already scolded ourselves for a hundred times over.

Mercy, mercy. Can we please give ourselves some mercy? You would consider anyone who spoke to you like this to be abusive!

Some people resort to deprivation ("you can't have that, you don't deserve it"), or confine themselves, or physically hurt themselves.

I don't know exactly what it is like for you, but you know. Maybe you reprimand yourself like a boot-camp drill sergeant. Maybe you don't give yourself any credit for all the good things you do. Maybe you worry relentlessly, stressing yourself sick. And yet you're still here. And you're "just fine," aren't you?

Whether it's your weight or the need to make more money or exercise more, these are all situations that don't require negativity or self-judgment to affect a change. Even when we admit that we can't torture ourselves into changing, we continue to do it. In this miserable concept, you cannot accept yourself. You can't give yourself a "thumbs up." When there's little to no personal support or love, there's usually not enough self-care.

What if every time you catch yourself saying something like, "Hah, look what you did. How stupid!" you hug yourself, bring yourself some love, and say something kind to yourself, like, "You did a great job! You did your best and your best is good enough. You're really working hard on this goal. Do you need some water, a nap, or a walk?"

My time to clobber myself is while I'm driving. My mind tells me that I said something really dumb or that I screwed up an important task. I have a rule: The moment I catch it, I refuse to allow the self-flogging to continue. I say, "Cindy, you're a really good person. What a great person you are! I love you."

This is my formula for short-circuiting my own style of personal torture. I keep affirming my personal value until these messages sink in and soften me into self-love. It works every time. Feel free to use these lines or formulate your own.

As for making positive, lasting change in my life, I aim to try new things with extra loving kindness like I'm helping a toddler take her first steps. I use patience and persistence and take those small steps forward. Reward yourself in healthy ways. Drop the drill sergeant's voice. That never works for long.

Another tip to consider: Do what you do because it brings you joy and self-love, not from a place of fixing some inner state of "not enough." When you immerse yourself in joyful activity, you experience the rewards immediately. When you try to fix some perceived deficiency, no amount of achievement will give you the satisfaction you truly desire.

Ask yourself what personal quality you are really craving within your goals. Keep going after your goals, but give that quality to yourself right now. Not everything you do will be pleasant, but you can still do those things with love. You can also do something that you know provides the quality you seek. Choose a task that makes you feel confident, competent, secure, and buoyant.

Affecting change in your life with love is far healthier and may yield better results. It's more likely to create better neural pathways in the brain. Positive energy grows things; negative energy depletes them.

My friend Mary invited me to hike Mount Whitney with our friend, Susan. They were both singers. Mount Whitney is a daunting 14,460-foot climb, the highest mountain in America's Pacific Northwest. It's usually a two or three-day hiking adventure, but many have accomplished it in one day, provided they begin at 2am in the morning.

Our climb was intense, but we found ourselves floating up

that mountain past others who looked overly tired. In reflection, our trek seemed effortless because we sang the whole way! We harmonized with each other. I would hum along when I didn't know the words. It made for a fun time! We sang our hearts out up that mountain, all day long, while the others trudged along, head down. Some caught our happy vibe and smiled at us. Others looked away as they dragged themselves up methodically. One guy didn't make it; rangers carried him down the mountain on a stretcher. The air gets thin at that altitude and can cause serious problems. I share this story to show the significance of staying positive when tackling a challenge.

In another context, I know from skiing black diamond runs that staring down a snowy chute at the summit of a windblown mountain top can bind your stomach in knots and send a rush of fear through your veins. I can sense the fear in the air from others psyching themselves up for the launch, as I prepare myself to ski down the run. At this moment, I think of a song and wait until I feel a lift of happiness, then I descend.

This deliberate shift from contracted fear to delightful joy sends a different pulse in my body. I am confident that I have the knowledge and experience needed to make precision curves down the steep decline. But it's the vibration of positive energy that is most needed to execute what I know.

In hindsight, it is obvious that my buoyant, positive attitude helped me triumph on the steep ski slope and the long climb up Mount Whitney. I was not only physically fit, I was free from the negative ramblings of my mind, from the focus on my aching legs, and from the fear that we wouldn't make it to the top and back down before dark.

Where thought goes, energy flows. If I had let worries fester, I could have lost precious energy. I might have worked myself up into some torturous state of worry over not making it down the mountain. We were late getting back and had to walk the last hour in very low light. This could have caused a twisted ankle.

 Any number of things can go wrong when we allow a negative, self-absorbed mind to run wild. Bringing emotion to our thoughts can magnetize negativity. The mind starts reacting to our own stories as if they are real. And that is a slippery slope indeed.

Since thought is creative; you can use your mind to help you. Try singing or dancing to your favorite music to lift you out of self-torture mode and to assist you with any challenge.

When we hear our favorite songs, we return to our hearts. One of my girlfriends starts her day with her favorite tunes,

and creates her own morning exercise dances! She starts slow, then escalates her movements until she glistens with bliss and laughter. What a great way to bring the whole body, emotions, and mind into a positive flow!

Try your own kind, positive, encouraging self-talk. Try humor! You can shift almost any unnerving situation in life by bringing humor into it. If you exaggerate an unwelcome notion into absurdity, you can more easily laugh it off. The incongruity between reality and what we think about it is where comedy comes from. If I can't find the humor in a situation, I picture a scene from a movie that really makes me laugh.

When we attack ourselves, we are in our heads fueling an ugly concept about who we are. Sometimes that voice is an echo of our parents' feeble and sometimes cruel attempts at discipline. They likely stopped doing that long ago, but we have taken over this flogging! Again, whenever you catch yourself in cruel self-punishment, remember that you have options. Try turning it into a kind voice. Or, simply say, "I love you" in the middle of whatever mental storm is happening.

This statement can return you to the present moment. And your awareness handles the rest.

Another step out of this harmful concept is to become the soft voice of the wisest, most loving parent you can imagine. Let this voice speak instead of the mean, critical one. No one can give you the comfort you need better than your own conscious adult self. Kindness comes from within.

Exercise: The 10-second kindness cure for most problems.

The heart is Home. It is where peace is. It is the place of love, and safety. Take a deep fresh breath, then lightly touch your heart. Take another slow enjoyable breath, as slow as you can, while imaging love filling and flowing all through you. Then let go as you breathe out. Take in one more even slower breath, as if the air smells of the sweetest ambrosia. Breathe out with an audible sigh, for good measure. Tune in to the energy you feel, reveling in these last exquisite moments. Notice the silence. Stay in this blessed place until you are complete.

The more you do this, the more you will create in yourself a centered and calm, peaceful presence. You can bring these qualities with you into your day, every day.

* * *

All the suffering in the world involves people trapped in a concept. Cruelty of any kind is of the ego. Someone who hurts another must be totally disconnected from the human before them, and fully lost in a hellish mental concept filled with misunderstandings and justifications. Such is the insanity of living based on concepts alone. I doubt anyone would say they like war and all its atrocities, but we can be that warlike, that unconscious, and that cruel to ourselves and to each other.

Fighting and self-torture are two of the many awful ways we allow concepts to harm our lives. Concepts are arrogant in that they believe they are the truth and the whole truth. They don't look twice. They are selfish in their intentions. And they are fixed, unchanging.

I'll say categorically that concepts are *always untrue* because they only reference the content of the past and the future and don't exist in the potent, living present. Concepts are cold and hard because they live in the head and don't let the heart's wisdom become involved. When you are in the present moment, you are connected to your heart, which is connected to Source. Loving compassion, wisdom, kindness, and positive action will always accompany you when you are present. In this moment, even when you don't have all the answers, you can deeply know that you have all you need.

Thank you for being more kind to yourself, more tolerant of others, and more praising of each other. One way to return to personal kindness is to recall all the things you have accomplished in your life, big and small. You have contributed so much good to this life; every act of kindness has lifted your karma.

As I recommended, get a notebook and write down these contributions. When you keep an ongoing list of all your blessings, your gifts, your wins, and your achievements, you return your focus to the positive. This list will remind you of the many good things in your life when you're feeling down. This journal is also where you keep your issue-solution log that leaves no struggle dangling without transforming it with new insights and different ways to support you. Dwell on these positives to bring you back to the proper perspective— you really are brilliant, unique, accomplished, wise, capable, and loveable.

7   EXTREME LIMITATION
FOR NO REASON AT ALL

This type of concept doesn't offer any worthwhile benefit from a self-imposed limitation, such as taking a therapeutic cold shower or limiting your intake of food. The self-imposed limitations presented below are arbitrary. They may seem too small to be concerned about, but if you have thousands of them, they add up to a strict and grim lifestyle for no reason at all.

You might imagine that extreme limitation for no reason at all is being in boot camp or traversing the African Sahara, but even these endeavors have their benefits. This definition of extreme limitation is having a multitude of *unnecessary* rules about what we should and shouldn't do that bring us no real value.

We impose extreme limitations on ourselves every day. We don't need walls to confine us when our own minds are perfectly capable of doing the same job. We do it through our extremely narrow definitions of how to live.

For example, you don't skip down the street if you're an adult; those days are supposed to be long past. Polite people don't make eye contact longer than a nanosecond with strangers.

Another example of extreme limitation is the amount of emotion we are allowed to express. It's dreadful when a man cries out loud. It's unnerving when someone raises their voice past a certain level. No one is supposed to walk backwards or sing in certain places or fart or rip up money or lay down on commercial lawns or take the day off from work without being sick.

In this concept, everything must be done in a certain way. Also, you can't just do nothing. We worry over the smallest unimportant things like a hair out of place. We have our own rule book, and it is thick.

Extreme limitation involves a constant focus on lack. Although we live in a rich, multi-diverse culture able to enjoy modern conveniences, luxuries, and options, we fixate on scarcity. We belabor the lack of jobs for our college graduates or the soaring price of goods or whether we'll have our social security benefits years from now. We could have an audience of 75 people filling an auditorium, but we brood over those 25 vacant seats.

Extreme limitation can be insincerity. It's as subtle as automatically answering "fine" when someone asks, "How are you?"

Living in extreme limitation is when you've become your façade, your persona. It is the role you play in life that you've mistaken for your true identity. When you become a role or imitate a role model, you aren't fully you. Your language becomes jargony. You assume mimicked expressions. Your beliefs are more dogma than wisdom.

The sad thing is that people don't realize they prefer the comfort of a little box called "this is ok." Venture beyond that small existence or transgress the smallest rule, and our alarms scream as if we're escaping prison.

No one is reprimanding us. We do it to ourselves. In your own life, ask yourself if you are willing to become a little freer to live without needless rules. Notice how many beliefs you have around the wrong way to live. Notice how habitual and repetitious your life has become, or how much time you spend focusing on a few negatives despite the vast number of positives in your life.

Try to break through a few needless limitations! Put your toilet paper roll on the other way. Go to a different grocery store. Rearrange your living room furniture and the direction of your bed. Relax the urge to stay in task-master mode when you could go take a walk in the park. Break through your extreme limitations in personal exchanges. You could smile at someone for just a moment longer. You may just catch the gift of their smile and enjoy a sweet conversation.

We have so much good in our lives. We can focus on ways to stay positive, and we can override those pesky prompts that whisper in our ear that we broke a rule. Once we do, we'll see that there is so much more to focus on in our amazing lives than remaining in extreme limitations for no reason at all.

8   HOW WE CAME UP WITH ALL THESE IDEAS

It really doesn't matter where all our concepts come from if we realize they simply aren't true, are not who we are, and don't serve us. This realization can always interrupt and dispel the lies of the past we grew up believing. Having said that, it's time to dive into two primary origins that gave rise to our limiting concepts: family of origin and commercial marketing.

For example, Mom is afraid—all the time. She's afraid you'll catch a cold and miss a meal on the way to being hit by a bus. She misconstrues her fear as loving concern, and she offers a heaping spoonful of warnings that can become a bit annoying: "Are you Ok? Are you sure? Did you get enough to eat? Have you packed everything? Please wear a jacket or you'll catch a cold!" She thinks these worries make her a good mother.

Many of us buy into the concept that worry is a thoughtful emotion, but how would you feel if I replace the phrase, "I just worry about you" with "I don't trust you or your ability to figure things out completely. Nor do I trust that you are safe and that things will work out."

Now how do you feel about the "thoughtfulness" of worrying?

We are exposed to worry from the get-go. By 30 years old, we've been duly warned about the perils and pitfalls of life in a million ways. Heeding all this worry is like accepting a noose tied around our necks and living as if life truly is terrifying. It is to peer over the edge of a cliff focusing on the ravine and never looking forward to the bridge that awaits. Always worried, we lock up safe and sound when we could be spreading our wings to fly.

Worry is not a supportive energy. Notice when you are around someone who worries. To this crazy concept, counter with, "Thanks so much for your concerns and warnings, but I trust in myself and my abilities. I've got this!"

Some of our handed down crazy concepts *were* true and helpful at a time in life, but they no longer apply. One example of this is adhering to roles for males and females. Women's careers are no longer limited to teacher, nurse, secretary, or flight attendant. Mothers aren't the only parent responsible for raising a child. More fathers are choosing to be the family's stay-home parent while moms assume the role of head of household and bread winner. All children can and should play with all toys whether cars, balls, dolls, bugs, or flowers. Every color of the rainbow belongs to both genders. When we open ourselves up to more choices, we break free from the stereotypes our predecessors were restrained within.

"Don't talk to strangers! Don't quit your job even if you hate it! Don't throw that screw away; you may need it!" These hand-me-down messages are based in lack and fear. Handed down by our loving, well-meaning parents, they mistakenly become tradition.

My parents were post war babies. They both went through a time of extreme poverty after losing their fathers when they were pre-teens. The lack of money created a hoarding strategy to get by. Many decades later, my parents still hoard albeit in a very organized manner that hides this unnecessary concept. Keeping collections that aren't actively used and enjoyed is another crazy useless concept. To be more concept-free, you are charged to drop any useless pastimes from our well-meaning parents.

It's Ok to break traditions that don't make sense. We can trust our own instincts to decipher between outdated habits, what to maintain, and what to throw away.

As for mom's hand-me-down worries, we know the difference between irrational fears and actual danger. If the situation feels right (and you'll know the difference), leave the house without a coat! Clutter-clear your home to keep only what you use. Doing this gives you more energy and an organized efficient set of belongings.

As for Mom and Dad, whether they are around or not, whether they earned it or not, our job is to love them, realizing they were carrying around concepts passed down from their parents who received passed-down concepts as well.

As we awaken out of this repeating pattern from our lineage, we are privileged to break this cycle forevermore. With our newfound clarity, we can forgive our dear folks who just wanted the best for us.

*   *   *

The second main origin of our concepts comes from the marketing and advertising industry. Companies spend trillions of dollars to sell us products, services, viewpoints, and beliefs. This entire industry is booming because selling us things makes shareholders huge money.

Even if we learned to be suspicious of advertising, good sense goes out the window when all those attractive people are having a wonderful time while using a particular product. It's hard to remember that certain food isn't good for us when it's associated with images of gorgeous partners running together across a beach. We should realize that slim models on the screen don't really fill their bellies with what they sell. Hopefully, we start to notice the difference between our appetites and our nutritional needs.

Advertising can be sneaky. Many ads incorporate subliminal messages using the carrot that you'll have great sex or financial success if you buy their products. If an image flashes on screen at $1/37^{th}$ of a second, the subconscious mind takes it in as fact without the conscious mind ever seeing it!

It takes conscious, deliberate thought and discipline to see through the subterfuge. Always remember that advertising preys on our weaknesses using false promises. Further, the subconscious cannot differentiate between truth and falsehood, and it hears all statements in the positive. For example, if you dwell on not eating sugar, avoiding sugar, and choosing sugar-free things, your subconscious mind only hears "sugar, sugar, sugar." And what you focus on long enough, attracts!

The fashion industry pushes the crazy concept that females aren't slim enough if they don't look like movie stars or the supermodels in magazines and commercials. The diet industry also pushes this crazy concept by selling us pills and diet food filled with chemicals that don't help you lose weight. The plastic surgery industry provides elective procedures that scrub and cut our faces. They advertise the crazy concept that a puffy set of lips is a more desirable look.

Our children are not safe from marketing propaganda. Barbie dolls were made with impossible dimensions. If Barbie was human-sized, she would stand 5 feet 6 inches tall, weigh 110 pounds, and have a 38-inch bust, 33-inch hips, and an 18-inch waist. Thankfully, Barbie dolls are being made with more realistic proportions than the original model.

The weight-loss industry counts on our weight to yo-yo from fad diets and processed packaged diet foods to continue its big income streams. It's crazy to believe that we should compromise our health in quick weight-loss schemes. Losing weight and maintaining our health requires a common-sense approach to reduce unhealthy food intake, a focus on modest portions of healthy food, and gradual increase of activity levels.

"Oh sure," you might say, "that's more easily said than done!" But instant gratification doesn't belong in the formula of weight loss. We are stuck believing, "Unless I look like someone else, I am not attractive and, therefore, I am not loveable." *We are already beautiful and wonderful just as we are,* no matter what these industries say. Our image in the mirror is going to change. If we don't feel and see our own self-love reflected back, no product, size, or surgery will change this. One key is to ask yourself why you are buying a particular product. Try to purchase from a place of joy and self-love, not to fix things your ego decides is wrong with you.

We can remain present to the immeasurable value of who we really are when making our choices.

If you make purchases in a well-rounded mindful way, if you read labels, and listen to your intuition, you'll navigate your way through these powerful marketing industries with more clarity. You can even have a measure of compassion for businesses that are just trying to make a living—and ignore the hype.

*　　*　　*

In nature, winter is a time of dormancy. Plants drop their leaves. Animals hibernate. For us, it's a time of slowing down, going inward, and reflecting upon the year that has passed. It's a perfect time for hot cocoa by a fireplace with a soft blanket and a good book.

We mimic this time of dormancy in some ways. Schools take a winter break. Many people go on winter vacations. But for the most part, we are bombarded by another type of crazy concept that befalls the winter season: a commercialized set of holidays.

We, as Americans, are steered towards being holiday consumers. We push our way through traffic and stand in lines at various department stores to buy loads of gifts for everyone. We overindulge in sweets and attend many parties. Because of the massive marketing efforts we've come to know, we buy our way through Christmas.

Sure, it's wonderful to see presents wrapped under a tree on Christmas morning, especially when creating this magic for the little ones in your family. However, the industry has highjacked Christmas! They pump a consumer holiday upon us to such a degree, it turns too much of our focus on materialism. Our finances are ravaged. We go into high credit card debt. The true meaning of Christmas and our Holy days can easily get lost.

The way back from holiday craziness to holiday richness is to contemplate our own values and our own true meanings of the holidays, then stay in the spirit of why we're coming together.

Before heading into your next holiday season, decide what qualities you wish to experience. Then bring these qualities, such as peace, balance, and compassion to everyone you encounter.

This intention can sidestep much drama, rushing, and superficiality that often is the root cause of the sadness many feel around the holidays. We can enjoy a deeper, more enriching, and peaceful wintertime. We can reinvent our true meaning of the seasons.

When we focus on the miracles all around us and on common kindness, our connections become gentle. We can align with nature and slow down and turn inward. If you are religious, you can change a materialistic holiday into a holy one by honoring its historical significance.

Attempts from the marketing and advertising industry may not persuade us any longer as we wake up from a marketed presentation of the holidays that isn't our own. We need not feel guilty about changing our traditions to honor ourselves. We can give our family the gift of dropping consumerism madness and embracing a new holiday tradition, one that is more meaningful and enjoyable, one that speaks to our soul.

9 KICKING IT INTO GEAR WITH RESOLVE

When I was twenty-three, I worked as a receptionist for a mortgage company. I wasn't happy there in my entry level job. One day at an office party, I overheard my boss telling my plus-one guest, "Cindy? She will never go anywhere." Wow, what an eye opener that was! It was a real gift to overhear this gossip because it gave me the adamant resolve to do just the opposite.

Soon after, I searched in the *Common Ground*, a spiritual magazine for massage schools in Berkeley, CA. I found what I thought was the best course for my needs. I enrolled in a 15-day intensive. It was 10 hours per day for 15 straight days. And it gave me a lifetime certification to practice Massage Therapy in the state of California upon completion.

I scheduled my two-week paid vacation during this schooling.

Halfway through, I quit my job. I had rent to pay, a car payment, credit card bills, and another week of my massage education to finish. I had no clients, equipment, or income.

I trusted the process and finished. To my great delight, I managed to get just enough paying clients by the end of the month to cover my bills. Then I never looked back.

This is how I launched what became a thirty-year, thriving, financially successful and fulfilling career. I leaped into the spiritual path of the healing arts. This occupation filled my heart and soul with purpose. But I knew I had to risk everything, trust in myself against all odds, and take swift bold action steps to affect this change.

I discovered that the way to my true path is to find something that brings me joy. From the first day of my training, I was like a lightbulb, bright and super-charged. The energy and enthusiasm I felt was a clear sign that I was on my true path. When you contemplate what path to take in life, look to your excitement level. Excitement is the sign that can lead you to your truest path, one that aligns with your talents, needs, and sense of fulfillment. Excitement is the energy that will magnetize the right people, places, and supportive tools to you. Joyful excitement brings a sense of effortlessness to your work.

Take time to journal a few things that get you excited. Let ideas percolate. Your excitements, however small, can become the faithful and trustworthy guide to a worthwhile life path.

I can hardly imagine what my life would have become if I hadn't made that abrupt, courageous change, or worse, if I had believed what my boss said about me. I might have remained an underappreciated receptionist or drifted into another go-nowhere job, collapsed from believing someone else's low opinions of me.

As discussed in Chapter 3, a defeatist attitude is pure poison. You'll see little upside to playing it safe, doubting yourself, and remaining small. If you are ready to make a big change, identify what makes you really fed up with your current situation, then build that discontent until you have a burning resolve to do something different, something better with your life! This could be your big moment to fulfill a dream and set out to make it happen!

When my boss put me down that night, I was outraged, incensed, insulted. Honestly, I was freaking pissed off. "What a betrayal," I thought at the time. Or was it?

I eventually became grateful for that cruel comment because it jarred me awake. It was the impetus that launched my successful, happy career. Besides, maybe he was right; maybe I *was* acting like a go-nowhere employee. That doesn't matter. What matters is I used adamant resolve to give me the will power, determination, and guts to grab that rope and swing elsewhere. I flew up and away into my dream career!

Let's be clear about something. Adamant resolve is similar to, but not the same as anger or rage. Anger in its healthy expression is a reaction to a violation. Anger's true underlying emotion is sadness, which is a lower vibration than anger because it is debilitating. On the other hand, anger says, "How dare you? Something must be done about this, darn it!" Anger burns a lot of energy. It is a perfectly healthy emotion if you channel it, or feel it and then let it go. Anger becomes problematic when the ego wants to take charge of the fight, retaliate, and punish another for the harm caused. But often, the only harm was a pushed button. The person filled with anger *already* had a wound that was restimulated.

Acting out, yelling, launching cruel words, and throwing punches whether physically or verbally is poor anger management. This is how wars start, when our egos' crazy rationale justifies attacking another country rather than cooling off and seeking diplomatic resolutions. Bitterness perpetuates because unconscious ego-driven angry people don't use these tools.

What would have come of the situation with my gossiping boss if I'd told him off, announced that I overheard his horrible remarks against me, and then called him a jerk? Anger when in your ego, can burn like a forest fire. This type of anger causes us to attack. It causes long standing resentments and much damage to all.

The way out of this vicious downward spiral is to turn it into personal and powerful resolve. Realize that there's always a pearl of truth in the matter that angers us. That pearl for me was that I saw I was being an under achiever. Realize that the person you're really mad at is yourself! Ask, "What's my unlearned lesson that caused this?"

If you use your anger to blame, punish, or control a person or situation, that's abuse. That usually backfires and escalates the drama. Instead, consider what adamant resolve does! It brings solutions.

The solution to shifting your anger into resolve lies in a curiosity about why you were disturbed. Then, the incredibly powerful energy of anger can funnel into your newfound ideas fanning the flames of your positive new life direction.

Further, once you accept responsibility for your anger and question what's *really* bothering you, you're back in your power. You can always expect some type of personal breakthrough. This is how adamant resolve works.

Teaming with energy, adamant resolve can be a vehicle for great personal change. Funnel all your discontent towards different solutions in your life. It does take a measure of humility and some contemplative work to do this, but when you do, it makes all the difference.

Seek to reinterpret tragedies for their silver linings, their unexpected gifts. If you don't, what's the point? Is it to enforce a belief that life is nothing but a series of problems? How depressing.

Notice how complacency becomes the bigger tragedy. We know where that leads—off the path of new open horizons and back into our comfort zones. You can thank your ego for trying to help, but ego has no place being involved when you are angry, because it believes in taking revenge. It wants to judge; it wants to repeat your victim story at every opportunity. It wants to become even more angry, as if any of these crazy strategies help the situation. We all know that following the ego's prompts in anger can lead to a mountain of drama, hurt feelings, and pain. Let's choose differently.

Instead of falling for the ego's crazy concepts, let yourself feel your anger. Once you experience and honor your anger, let it pass through you without harm. When you're ready, ask for an insight from the anger.

Sometimes tragedy gives us a powerful new perspective. When someone dies, in your despair, you notice how temporary everything is and how much the people around you matter. This is how *M.A.D.D., Mothers Against Drunk Driving*, was formed. The bereft mother of her high school child who was killed in a car crash by a drunk driver founded this organization. Today, better awareness about the deadly risks of drunk driving has saved countless lives. This extreme example shows how people can take the worst situations and redirect their energy in positive life affirming ways from the experience.

Regardless of the reason for your anger, you can use this emotional energy to catapult yourself into a promising change. Adamant resolve moves mountains!

When it's time to make that move, proceed with faith and trust. Miracles happen when you have conviction in your actions. Top athletes like Michael Jordan and Tiger Woods execute their sport in full faith, without worry or hesitation. They don't play it safe. They are "in the zone," fully present and single-minded during that swing or free throw.

Allow yourself to practice any type of behavior change this way. When you show up and drop all thoughts, you are a conduit of energy, a channel for skill and mastery. This is how you reach new heights! Amazing things can happen when you decide to side-step the outrage, the blame, and the fight.

One more idea on taking concept-free action: don't wait until everything is just right and situations are perfect to move forward. The perfect appointed time doesn't exist. Try to handle issues *during* the process of taking action. It's not necessary to eliminate all your fears beforehand. Don't let fear stop you. *Feel the Fear and Do It Anyway* is the title of a classic book by Susan Jeffers that says it all. The experience of fear almost never goes away. All winners face their fears and proceed anyway. Doing so, you can expect a rush of excitement and the satisfaction earned from going for it.

Great accomplishments have occurred by average, every-day folks because of adamant resolve. You stop procrastinating and start working out. You go back to school and get that long awaited degree. You get good and fed up with your weight. I used adamant resolve to eliminate my pesky food cravings!

Adamant resolve is a massive positive force you can channel to launch change in your life.

10 CONCEPTS ABOUT MONEY

You can't out-give God, but you can under-give God.

This statement refers to the idea that what we give out comes back multiplied. This is a universal Law. Abundance multiplies and, unfortunately, so does lack. When we freely contribute, when we help one another, volunteer, work, and extend our efforts, we receive amplified returns. If we hold back, don't help others, hoard, and stop working, this lack of effort multiplies scarcity in our lives.

The ever-abundant energy of God is limitless. The more we contribute, the more we are replenished. Only we limit how much money we choose to circulate. If, in an error of thinking, we hold back to have more, the consequence is more lack.

When you view money as an opportunity to express a valuable cooperative exchange, you can more easily spend it. It is wise to save money and use a budget to ensure your self-sufficiency. Having a positive regard for money management allows you more peace.

Instead of feeling resentment when you pay your bills, connect the dots to the enjoyment and security you receive in your home and in your affairs. Then, paying these bills becomes a time of gratitude for the heat, the food, and the easy removal of waste that faithfully supports you. Remember, what you send out comes back to you. Mentally saying "Thank you" during each exchange brings more positive energy to the circumstance. See money as the vehicle that transports this exchange of kindness.

Alternatively, experiencing a hard time around money indicates that you have some judgments about it, a poor history with it, or don't feel good about spending it. As a result, the circulation slows down. It becomes stagnant.

When giving feels bad, exchange becomes a negative experience for both parties. No one wants to be the recipient of hard feelings, lack, ambivalence, and resistance. Therefore, receiving money becomes harder. This cycle repeats, furthering bad feelings and the concept that money itself is the problem. It causes other concepts to form such as "money is hard to come by," and worse, "money is the root of all evil."

One crazy money concept we could eliminate is being "penny wise and pound foolish." Here's how silly we are: We analyze each gas station for the lowest price, sometimes driving way out of our way, to save a few pennies per gallon on gas. Then we'll go out to a nice restaurant and order a bottle of wine at $48 followed by $37 dinners totaling almost $150 after the tip. This is for just one meal for a couple. Then we'll grab a few things at the grocery store the next day and refuse the bag for our items to save ten cents.

Be pound wise and penny frivolous!

*　　*　　*

I attended "Secrets of the Millionaire Mind," a 3-day seminar by T. Harv Ecker. He led the class through exercises to analyze our beliefs around money. The exercises aimed to weed out our unconscious negative beliefs about money and redefine success in positive new terms. I created my "financial blueprint," and I learned how couples can create a joint blueprint to manage their shared financial life from the same page of understanding.

Class members took a pre-test at the beginning and a final test at the end of class on our beliefs about money. After taking the final test, we were astonished by the differences in our money beliefs from just a week prior. We let go of many erroneous concepts around money that were no longer true for us.

This course, in one weekend, dramatically shifted my awareness around the truths, the fallacies, and the potency of money. The shift in my attitudes and concepts about money allowed me to start making different choices. I began attaining wealth unencumbered by my previous flawed thoughts that were stopping my flow.

To boot, the course was completely free. I highly recommend taking "Secrets of the Millionaire Mind," if it's still available. If not, read T. Harv Eker's book, *The Millionaire Mind*. It's a worthwhile read and a life-changer.

Here are some tips and pointers for handling money:

- Appreciate and respect your money. Say "Thank you" when you obtain it. Bless it when you spend it.

- Stack your currency in ascending order, facing the same direction. Flatten the kinks. Interestingly, those with judgements on money wad it into weird shapes making it hard to count. You can lose money without a clear system of organization.

To have a huge breakthrough around your relationship with money, do the following life-changing exercises.

1) In your journal, list the judgments you have about money. Leave ample writing space after each judgment, at least a line or two.

2) List your judgments about rich people. After these judgments, leave some space.

3) Write a *neutralizing greater truth* about each judgment. Keep writing positive truths *until the judgment is no longer true for you*.

4) When any new judgment around money comes up for you, write it down and follow step 3.

This exercise weeds out the crazy damaging concepts that stand in the way of you attaining wealth. The goal is to eliminate your negative concepts about money so you can allow more prosperity into your life. Also, take the time to remove all the toxic negative assumptions around wealthy people, so you can become one of them! Because who would want to become, let alone associate with, anyone you harbor such negative judgments about?

Once you finish these exercises, expect to live with more ease and comfort around money. The greater truths you embrace bring power, clarity, organization, and respect to the flow of money in your life, therefore increasing your abundance. Eliminating your negative, crazy financial concepts enables you to live in more power and ability and ease to do what you wish with your time.

Once you create a positive relationship with money, weed out your negative beliefs, and put some organization in place, you can move on to creating other good habits such as paying off your credit cards and saving your cash for larger expenditures like cars and vacations.

There are many classes on mastering money, plenty of which you can sign up for online. Without learning a base structure and some good practices, money can fall through your fingers.

It's a personal triumph to have financial security at any level of achievement. It's not what's most important, but it sure helps us enjoy all the fruits of life. I don't think I've ever done an exercise that's been more tangibly satisfying and monetarily more effective. I welcome your emailed feedback and success stories from doing this work.

Know that we live in an abundant world teaming with resources and financial opportunities. The power to create what you want lies within you and is always within reach. Wishing you a more powerful concept-free relationship with money.

11 LOOKING VS. SEEING

One sunny afternoon while watering my plants, a remarkable thing happened to me. I popped into a higher state of awareness.

It was warm out. I know it's best to water before 10 AM or after the sun goes down. The water droplets on a plant at midday can become little magnifying glasses that burn the plants. But I was firmly stuck in a concept of not having any other time to water my plants other than midday.

I took two 2-gallon sprinkler buckets filled to the brim to my landscape as it doesn't have a drip system. I began watering my drought-tolerant bushes I'd planted a year ago.

Because the bushes tended to splay, I could see the base of the plant. I mentally asked where I could give the plants the best dose of water. As I sent a nice spray of water across the thirsty vegetation, I felt a shock of cold as if I'd just stepped into an ice-cold shower. Then I felt a sense of satisfaction coming from the location of its main root system. I knew where the root was under the ground. I *sensed all this from the plant!*

Marveling at this fascinating heightened perception, I practiced it on the rest of my plant friends. I felt the same cold brisk water again, then I kept watering until I sensed a water-logged feeling.

Plants have a nervous system; I know this from Biology 101, but I didn't add two and two together to deeply realize that they can *feel!* This day, I could feel in real time what the plant was feeling.

To my surprise, the plants were all talking to me in the language of emotions and sensation. One rosemary plant was crying. Even after I gave it water, it cried. This was the type of rosemary that grows vertically. It had been sheered into a low dome shape. It hurt from this and cried from being cut down too much! Intuitively, I raked its aromatic straight branches softly with my fingers and sent it soothing sounds. I made a mental note to tell the gardeners not to trim the rosemary down so much. Wow! What an experience!

Still reveling in my newfound "spidey-senses," I continued tending the plants around my yard. I consciously acknowledged each plant. As I turned toward the next, I heard: "Wait, you looked, but you didn't *see* me."

Whether this was the plant itself or my inner guidance or my imagination, I don't know. But I clearly heard, "Looking is two-dimensional, like viewing an image on a piece of paper. Looking is glancing, then searching your history for past similarities. Then, you project or impress these impressions onto what you're looking at. Looking misses most of it.

For example, maybe you notice a plant similar to one that grows in Grandma's yard, so you associate this plant with your feelings about Grandma. This is looking. You are not seeing the *plant*. You are super-imposing Grandma, her yard, her personality, and other impressions about her onto the plant you're viewing.

We do this with people too. We have a bundle of past impressions about people, some entirely erroneous. When we think we are looking at them, we are really seeing our own past opinions and judgments this person reminds us of. Therefore, looking is being lost in concepts. When you're in your concepts, there's little to no connection happening.

Truly *seeing* a plant or a person is sensing and connecting with its life force. Seeing involves an immersion in the moment. You will also feel a sense of loving compassion, because true *seeing* connects through the heart. People who are in love really *see* each other. Because they are fully present, life appears in vivid color. Their beloved is gorgeous because they are viewing through the eyes of unconditional love. Also, when you look deeply at someone, you can experience their soul, the source of their depth and true beauty." I stood there fascinated at this stream of insight.

It's a wild ride to go from looking at a plant, to talking to it, to feeling its magnificent life force, personality, and hearing its messages! But as hard as this is to believe, this happened to me. More wise words came to me:

"Everything is alive; true *seeing* is directly interfacing with life and noticing its multi-dimensional magnificence."

Looking is a function of the ego. The ego will look for what it can gain from the exchange, even when appreciating beauty, the ego takes. Looking at something reduces its value to its use. If an object of the ego's attention isn't seen as personally beneficial (a weed for example), it is rejected, discounted, then pulled out by its roots. This is what we do in life when we are living from our ego. This is how we relate to others when we look at them.

All living things need us to pierce through the illusion of looking into the beautiful capacity of *seeing* for more meaningful and compassionate connections.

We've stamped a false identity on the face of everything. Just under this is a luminous life waiting to be noticed. Alive, it is animated. It is an expression of love. The miracle of life is always before us, waiting for us to notice.

*   *   *

Exercise 1: Connecting with Plants

First "look" at a plant or a tree and list your observations, judgments, and any past associations with it. Next, set these lists aside and make this plant's actual acquaintance, like when you extend your hand to meet someone new. Focus on the vibratory life force of the plant and be receptive to sensations or qualities. Send this plant your love, become quiet, and wait for a response.

Ask, "Show me what I don't know about you." Then sense, feel, and hear whatever you can. Become even more quiet and receptive. Send it more love. Become one with it. Notice what you can sense.

Here is the formula for going from looking to seeing: Try it again, perhaps with a pet.

1) Notice any judgments and past associations with it

2) Say "Hi."

3) Notice its energy, tune into the sensations you feel.

4) Send love.

5) Quiet your mind and become receptive.

6) Send love again.

7) Notice what comes back.

If you practice this, you will be on your way to a whole new relationship with life, one that will bring you richness, sweetness, kindness, and a deeper connection with life. This type of energetic exchange will leave you in awe every time.

Exercise 2: Connecting with People

Try a similar activity with a person or a group of people and notice all the judgments that come up. Consider a stereotype you might be aware of. This is not to be hard on yourself; it is to become more conscious of the instinctual and unavoidable judgments our egos always harbor.

Keep releasing judgments by asking, "Is this true?" If it is not, forgive it. They are all projections anyway.

A projection is an attitude, behavior, or condition that we find unacceptable about ourselves and can't personally own, so we see this in others.

When we cannot resolve the flaws in ourselves, the ego sees it as something going on with other people. To turn this around, ask, "what is it I need to forgive about myself?" Then forgive it, and it's melted into wisdom.

Exercise 3: Judgments

Every judgment is just a bunch of conceptual garbage. Each time you catch yourself in a judgment, ask yourself, "Can I see this in a different way?" Refuse to maintain critical judgments of others.

Compassion says, "I care about you. I want to know more about you. Tell me your story." Compassion softens your view of everyone and allows for more acceptance. It puts you on the same playing field with others. Living with compassion is living harmoniously.

By truly seeing, we replace all our concepts that come with looking. We become more concept-free in our relationships. When you can *see* without judgment, you remain peaceful. Remaining connected and judgement-free with others, you are more kind. Without judgements, you'll see more clearly. These are all benefits from mastering the art of *seeing*.

Keep repeating these exercises and life will never be the same. From a heart-centered state of connectedness, so much is possible.

12 THE BODY, YOUR WORD, AND SOURCE

Whatever struggle you find yourself in, if you take a moment to have a nice fresh breath, and feel the love that you are, you'll return to peace. If you can catch yourself whirling around in any concept and use the following exercises to snap out of it, you'll make it back to sanity in record time.

Try this one:

Become acutely present and listen to the sounds around you. See how many sounds you can hear right now, in 10 seconds.

Did you notice how quiet your mind became? You cannot think any thoughts while you are listening! We cannot do these things at the same time. If you are plagued by relentless, rambling chatter, apply the technique of focused listening to quiet your mind.

Here's another exercise to bring you out of a concept—focusing on your body's natural energy.

Find a comfortable position, become quiet, and notice the sensations inside your body. Can you feel tingling energy in your hands? In your legs? In your feet? See how much tingling energy you can feel all at once. If you cannot feel this body energy, try it laying down right after exercising.

Did you notice that you became more grounded and your mind calmed down? We stay too much up in our heads. This simple exercise rebalances us. It also aids in stilling the mind. You cannot become deeply aware of your body's energies and think at the same time. Try it!

Becoming aware of the sounds around you and getting in touch with the sensations within your body brings you to the present moment.

The ego will say, "Yeah, yeah, that's not important; I need you to think about *this*." However, it *is* important to practice stilling the mind, learning deeper listening skills, and becoming more keenly present to your body's energies.

Tuning in to your body is not only calming, it's healing. Your physical body is your biggest supporter. It circulates, beats, digests, sees, and hears. It faithfully does this 24/7 for many decades non-stop. Giving it your attention is greatly satisfying to the body. It is a great method of self-love.

Further, consistently tuning into your body and its discontent allows you to better respond to its needs. Are you thirsty? (We usually are dehydrated.) Have you given your body all the nutrition, vitamins, and minerals it needs? Have you exercised? Rested fully? Have you laughed today?

Staying aligned with your body will pay you ample rewards as you get older. You'll feel when your body is healthy and more closely track when it's not feeling well before it becomes sick. You'll know what type of pillow best supports your neck and which shoes support your arches.

We are largely oblivious to and negligent of our body's needs. We override its messages and use pain medication to tune out its signals when it cries out. Being separate from our body is living in a concept of avoidance and denial. It only takes some recognition, loving attention, and moderate amounts of care to reunite us with our greatest friend, our body.

If we are mentally focused, we aren't in our bodies, and we aren't fully present. Presence involves awareness of our whole being—body, heart, mind, and spirit. If we don't remain present to our body's changing needs, we may be *interested* in health while we continue being cruel to our body.

We can all agree that it's important to eat healthy, well-rounded meals over junk food. It is *far* more important to give it the emotional nourishment it needs. If you are in any doubt about how to care for your body, begin with love and compassionate attention. Loving our bodies with an ongoing routine of self-care will pay off manyfold for the rest of our lives.

When sharpening your skills of listening, try becoming deeply receptive to your higher Self. The mind may say, "Where is my higher Self? Where do I focus?" When practicing, I like to focus on my heart and the top of my head at the same time.

Our mind tries to take us towards some mental daydream. Sharpen your presence right then. When our minds chatter, we think we need to pay attention to every thought that sweeps in. We do not have to be at the mercy of our mind's every interruption. We must use the mind like a tool for what *we* choose to think about, not what it chooses.

If you truly listen to your thoughts, they aren't even helpful most of the time! Most of those mental interruptions derive from crazy concepts and tend to create fear, sadness, or anger. At the very least, these uninvited thoughts distract us from the peace we seek. The only way to discourage this habit is to become quietly present. To get there, keenly listen to the sounds around you and feel the sensations within your body. In each instance, notice how quiet and peaceful you become.

*   *   *

Another way to help quiet mental chatter is by meditating. Meditation is the most powerful avenue to becoming concept-free. Meditation, in any of its diverse forms, lowers stress and calms anxieties. It restores, renews, and heals you on all levels. It unwinds the trauma and the crazy concepts we carry around. It connects us with Source. It returns us to balance and peace. Meditation is a full reset.

Meditation reveals a deeper consciousness only available when we shut out the outer world. Meditation brings us to what is real and true beyond our surface minds. It connects us to our own higher knowing. Meditation is sustenance for the Soul.

A great 7-minute meditation practice:

1) Sit in a chair with lower back supported, spine tall,

shoulders dropped, and as relaxed as possible.

2) Use the acute listening skill for 10 seconds. See how many sounds you can hear.

3) Do the body awareness practice for another 10 seconds or until you notice tingling in varies body parts.

4) Then, sit or lie quietly and focus on the rise and fall of your breath for a few very slow breaths.

5) Imagine breathing Love into your heart and head for a few slow breaths.

6) Let go into the silence for 5 minutes longer, or until you feel complete.

7) Repeat this 7-minute meditation daily for 21 days. Notice the results.

This exercise may feel uncomfortable or seem like a waste of time. This is just your ego resisting a good thing! It tells you you're too busy for this. You may hear a heightened state of chatter and think you're moving backwards on the path. The ego will finally realize you are in charge, and will eventually become silent. Just continue meditating on schedule. Do it with compassion. Find a time that doesn't infringe on your schedule or anyone else's. Take this worthy challenge!

Gradually and powerfully, practicing meditation will help you move into a more concept-free existence.

Here's another powerful yet quick meditation to bring peace and clarity of mind.

Structured Breathing Meditation:

1) Sit in a chair with lower back supported, spine tall, shoulders dropped, and as relaxed as possible.

2) Breathe in for a count of 4.

3) Hold the breath in for a count of 2.

4) Breathe out for a count of 6.

5) Hold on the out-breath for a count of 2.

6) Repeat steps 2 - 5 for a few rounds. When it feels like enough, drop the counting and finish your meditation in silence until you feel complete.

Give yourself a gift. Give it a try.

*   *   *

Chanting, another type of meditation, involves repeating a phrase of sacred sounds designed to use sound and vibration to attain health and high levels of consciousness.

Many mantras originated in India and China. "Nam Myoho Renge Kyo" comes from Japan and is the Nishironan

Dishonan branch of Buddhism. My favorite chant, "Ek Ong Kar, Sat Nam Siri, Wahe Guru," is a chant from the Sikhs who practice Kundalini Yoga. The Hindu tradition believes the sound of "Om" contains the entire universe and is the culmination of all sound. It is said to be the first sound at the beginning of time and encompasses the present and future. "Om" is probably the most common of all chants.

Chanting works by sending sound currents through your body that vibrate your chakras, or energy centers. Activated chakras, like a tuning fork, release blockages, also known as issues or karma. I enjoy chanting because in addition to all this healing, it is similar to the joy of singing while engaging in a meditation practice.

Chanting in a group is even more powerful. Taking a meditation class can help you learn and progress in your practice. The group's energy can aid in your development.

When you chant or meditate or do a yoga work-out, try doing it devotionally from an open heart. To do this, simply become grateful. Remember becoming happy for no reason? Try becoming grateful for no reason during your practice, or any time of the day.

A Devotional Guided Meditation:

Drop into the exquisite, serene center of your being within your heart. Touch your heart area softly. Let a loving warmth build in this area. Imagine breathing into a most beautiful rose scent. Breathe in bliss. You can build devotion by thinking of people you are grateful for. Keep breathing in a rose scented bliss and imagine your heart growing to the size of a hot air balloon. Then, once you reach an expanded state, sit in this heart-opened place until you feel complete. Return to your day bringing this devotional vibration with you.

Practicing these meditation techniques is invaluable. Routinely becoming calm and quiet is the ultimate concept buster. Mastering the art of routine meditation enables profound and unparalleled benefits to you on every level of your being.

*   *   *

You may be wondering, "How will meditation help me make concept-free choices?"

Divine intelligence, not ego, is where we always want to make our choices from. Meditation helps us connect with this divine intelligence. We cannot receive higher wisdom for proper choices in life if we are spun out in dramas, battles, fear, or are consumed by distractions.

I believe we live in a multi-dimensional, friendly, and cooperative universe. Many spiritual writings state that we have angels ready to assist, protect, and guide us if we ask for this help. The caveat is we need to ask.

Prayer for Divine Assistance:

From a quiet heart-centered place, connect with God (or universal energy, or your angels, or your higher Self), and say something like the following.

"Beloved Source, bring me your light and your love. Help me align with divine wisdom and unconditional love. Reveal to me what to do, what to say, and to whom.

I claim ___(whatever you are praying for)___ with ease and grace. Grant me this for my highest good and for the highest good of all. I am so grateful.

Thank you.

So be it. And so it is. Amen."

You can begin your day powerfully by saying this every

morning. Decide the results and qualities you want, and claim them to arrive with ease and grace. When you say, "...and for the highest good of all," it ensures your request for yourself is not at anyone's expense; it ends up benefitting everyone.

A prayer like this when spoken with sincerity, has the power to manifest things for you. It causes no harm, and it calls in a concept-free beautiful existence. Pay attention to any positive changes in your life from repeating this prayer. Pay attention to how your life is enriched by meditating.

We either follow our heart and wisdom, or we follow our ego. There are only two paths. Is there any doubt which is more beneficial? One path contains the clarity, insight, balance, and love. The other path causes all the messes, the struggle, misunderstandings, and dramas in our lives.

*   *   *

How do you know when you are connected to God? One way to tell is through the sensation of excitement. Excitement tells you three things:

1) That a particular decision or path is who you are.
2) That this is the direction you should take.

3) That following in this direction will bring you the support you need, the resources, energy, and people. Being supported, this path will feel effortless.

Excitement is the energy that sets you vibrating with joy over something. Having excitement about something indicates that it is right for you, and that you should at least investigate that direction.

So why do we discount our enthusiasm? In almost every case, we believe some crazy concept over our gut instinct. For verification in life, we often say, "Give me a sign." Excitement is your sign! Feeling excited means you have found your path.

Alternatively, when God answers an inquiry with "no," we receive this message as a constriction, a heaviness, fatigue, or tightness. This is also your God-given sign! Heed it. Likely your higher Self is saying "not completely," "not yet," or "Hell NO!" Although easily misunderstood, contractions and sinking feelings are just as valuable signals as excitement is. Our job is to notice and take proper action on the messages we get from Source. It's helpful to check in on our gut sense before rushing headlong into a situation.

A "no" signal can indicate an issue on your otherwise correct path. Once you receive a "no," stop. Go back to the drawing board.

Realize that a "no" is just as positive a signal as a "yes" because they both are clarifying messages about your path!

Begin to listen to your body when you ask what to do, where to go, who to speak to, and when. Tune into yourself *after* you make a decision. I often have more clarity right after making a choice. "Whoops, that wasn't right." It's never too late, once you get a "no," to say, "Wait a minute, I changed my mind."

We always receive signals. Unfortunately, we don't always understand them, so we ignore all our messages of excitement and contraction. The only reason we don't change course when we feel massive contraction, or take action when we feel excitement, is because we're stuck in a concept. Don't underestimate the power of reason to discount our instincts. It's why we get off course and stay stuck for far too long.

*   *   *

Affirmations are a powerful way to manifest good in our life. Try the following statements. Circle the ones that have the most power for you. Then, formulate your own.

- Everything that happens to me serves my highest good. I just need to figure out how this situation serves me.

- I'm always taken care of. I never have to worry.

- Money flows easily to me. I live in abundance.

- I don't get sick anymore. Every day, I feel greater health.

- I love my amazing life! I am living my best life and making better choices every day.

- Life is great! I'm thankful for everyone in my life. I am supported by my loving friends. I am loved.

Write your own powerful affirmations and put them where you can read them every day. Say them out loud. These statements don't have to be your current experience; they can represent what you are calling in. If Source is all that is and you are one with Source, these powerful expressions *are* true! You might not have accepted it yet. If a statement doesn't feel true, rephrase it to feel more real. For example, "I am wealthy" may not be the case. You need to believe your statement. You could change it to, "Money is beginning to flow more easily into my life." Regardless of your current situation, declaring affirmations out loud strengthens them in your reality.

Here's a little secret I've come to notice in my life: When I state something out loud with utter certainty, and another hears it, this helps make it come true. The more you share your truth, the broader you create your reality.

Here's another tip to keep in mind: Don't speak what you *don't* want to perpetuate. Avoid sharing the negative things going on in your life. People go on and on about what's wrong in their lives, what they hate, who said what, and what they hope won't happen, all the while energizing the very situation they would rather not have. So don't say things like:

>"I'm broke."
>"Life sucks."
>"I never have any luck."
>"I'm bad at ..."
>"I can't ..."

Or any version of "Yes, but..."

Those statements go out into the Universe and manifest too.

Without realizing it, we use our sob stories and complaints to bond with others. This way of strengthening friendships has an ugly side of throwing someone under the bus.

It doesn't mean we can't ever vent our frustrations. Of course we can, yet, to escape the perpetuation of crazy concepts, we must sharpen the power of our word and speak in a different way.

Instead of declaring, I'm broke," try saying, "I'm currently immersed in job hunting, excited to find new avenues that make me happy!"

If you want a concept-free life, you must give up your complaints, grudges, excuses, and victim perspective. Despite appearance, remember that *everything serves your highest good*, including your challenges and setbacks. They are there to teach you something. You just need to learn what that is.

*   *   *

Complaining is a misuse of our personal power. It presumes that life happens *at* us, not *for* us. Drop the words, "But, only, never, just, should, have to, and can't" from your vocabulary. These are debilitating words containing the power to limit you by your own declaration.

A massage therapist never knows when the phone will ring to bring us our next client. As a massage therapist, I had a month so slow, I made only $420.00. My rent at the time was $400.00. Did I go around spreading that story to anyone? No way. Even when a roommate asked how my practice was going, I responded, "Great!"

It *was* great. I loved giving massages; I was in my dream career. Besides, I could pay the rent, and I had $20.00 left.

This was a scary situation. But even when things like this happen, we can view our challenges with a new perspective such as, "At any moment the phone will ring, and I'll make another $150.00!"

If I turned this situation into a huge problem and told all my friends, I'd have circulated the reality that I don't have enough clientele. Perhaps my friends would wonder what I'm doing wrong or assume I'm just not that good at massage. That might keep them from referring clients to me. Even if my income returned to normal the next month, the gossip remains in people's minds. Worry, doubt, and imaginings are perpetuated. Sharing your sob story is just not worth the negativity that it creates. Refraining from complaining allows our temporary struggles to pass by without harm. I knew I could attract more clients by staying in cheerful gratitude. And I did.

The crazy concept to dump our burdens on others only strengthens the grim circumstances we seek to release. If you need to vent (it happens), write about the situation in a private journal. This is a free and invaluable resource. If you still need to share, find a counselor. Speaking with a therapist is a good way to provide your own resolve and protect your valuable community. Those negative messages are hard, if not impossible, to dislodge from people's minds.

Have you ever told your family and friends horrible things about your partner when breaking up, then later reconciled with "the monster" you portrayed? Did you wonder why you no longer felt supported when new issues arose? It's usually far better to save your complaints for your journal or therapist; both are great listeners, and neither is invested in what will happen next.

Complaining, victimhood, and gossip are all crazy concepts! And now you know how to overcome them.

Your friends will appreciate hearing how you triumphed over an obstacle and what you learned in the process. You will appreciate noticing what makes you truly excited, the guidepost of your most sincere path.

13   WE MAKE IT ALL UP

"Making it all up" means that we decide what things mean, then we react to our own definitions. Problems arise when we interpret something as bad or not supposed to happen. The problem becomes more negative when we decide the situation is someone else's fault. Viewing life in this way is an improper perspective driven by crazy concepts that make us victims.

When we adopt a victim mentality, we assume faulty interpretations and fear-based strategies. We believe others are to blame for all the bad that happens to us. Our ego creates this limited view from the erroneous reality that it is always right. Locked into this paradigm, we assume that's just the way life is.

The ego is not bad; it is impossible to live without an ego. The ego is about our survival and safety. It just goes too far. It's an incompetent decision maker in most areas of our life.

We need to apply a broader perspective, which includes imagining how the problem might be for others, what's the best choices considering all involved, and how this is serving me by teaching me something I really need to know.

With these simple reflections on any situation, you can untie the knot and soften the problem, turning a negative situation into a positive one. Once you get good at considering the silver linings in your breakdowns, you can expect a breakthrough every time.

It's never comfortable navigating a problem. This is why people unconsciously deflect blame onto others. Doing so is living an unconscious life. Victimhood leads to suffering, lack, and feeling out of control. We, on the other hand, turn our focus inward. Letting go of our crazy concepts, we prefer a powerful "Aha" moment of clarity. With each valuable lesson learned, our life is enriched.

A Course in Miracles says that life is neutral and meaningless, and we give it all the meaning it has. We are "meaning-making machines" placing value on neutral things, people, and situations.

It's perfectly fine to determine what is valuable to us. Problems arise when we place a negative interpretation on things. ("This is awful. Life sucks. I can't. It's your fault. There's nothing possible here.") These are all faulty concepts!

We can become meaning makers with positive interpretations! We can say, "everything serves my highest good, including this. I'm fine no matter what happens out there. I got this." When you stay in the positive, you'll experience that life is either delighting us in incredible ways, or it is helping us grow by bringing us the lessons and messages we need.

Once we know this, we are free. Life is always serving our highest good. It's always a worthy and positive adventure.

This is the most important message in the book, so I'll repeat it:

We make up what things mean for us then react to the definitions we've placed on them. When we become conscious to the law that everything serves our highest good, we can determine how this struggle serves to teach us something valuable.

Ask, "What do I need to learn from this situation?" And, "What must I change about myself?" Discovering these insights give us beneficial information that forever changes our course in life. Applying this inquiry to all issues brings proper perspective. This process transforms all issues for us.

* * *

The insights we find from one struggle can benefit us in many areas of our life. For example, you get into a car accident:

Instead of focusing on the damage to your car, all your missed appointments, the amount of time and money you'll spend, and the fact that it was their fault (since they rear-ended you), you inquire, "What's the lesson for *me*, here?"

One answer could be that you were speeding (insight). You realize if you slow down, you'll be safer on the road (beneficial life change). You also realize that your high blood pressure is possibly due to rushing (second insight), so you decide to slow down in general (second beneficial life change). Then you think if you play relaxing music, your tempo will be slower, and you'll feel more relaxed throughout the day (third beneficial life change). When you slow down, you may notice more beauty, like the flowers in your neighborhood (third insight). You create some floral arrangements, making one for your house and one for work (fourth beneficial life change). This is how collecting insights from one problematic situation can positively flow into other areas of your life, benefiting you many times over.

Inquiry can also redirect you away from the anger, frustration, resentment, and stress of the auto accident. It brings you back to a calm, balanced, and clear perspective. It transforms your blind spots into wisdom and gratitude for a revealed pattern that now no longer runs you.

We are either living unconsciously at the mercy of our crazy concepts, or we're making conscious interpretations, living concept-free, and soaring into our best life! If we don't apply inquiry by asking, "What can I learn from this struggle?" we'll be likely to assume negative core beliefs, such as the following:

- "Life is a battlefield. Life is a struggle."
- "Life is hard."
- "I'm barely making it. It's impossible to get ahead."
- "I can't trust anyone."

These negative beliefs become the fertile conditions for our failures. It's better to create positive core beliefs and repeat affirmations to strengthen them in our reality.

- "This rough situation isn't my Source. I am. And I am a champion."
- "All is well, no matter how it appears to be out there."
- "I am lovable, loving, and loved."

Core beliefs are extremely powerful. They are like the trunk of a tree with branches leading to other beliefs. It's wise to create and maintain positive core beliefs. Here are some more to consider adopting:

- "I'm good at making money."
- "I love people and crowds; the more the merrier."
- "No matter how difficult things become, I always land on my feet."
- "Everything always turns out for the best and is taken care of in good time."
- "All is well with my Soul."

Gathering insights from our issues in life demonstrates that life always presents ways to help us. We then remain free to navigate life purposefully peacefully, and powerfully.

*   *   *

I juggle a few careers: massage therapist, property manager, writer, and mom. If I believed I couldn't wear more than one hat, I wouldn't. If I believed I didn't have the time to go on vacations, I wouldn't have enjoyed the scuba diving I just did. When we say, "yes" to our possibilities, the "how" seems to find a way to our doorstep.

I traveled to Mexico to write a different book[2] *Crazy Useless Concepts and Breaking Through Them* needed to come next. Living in the present moment and having faith in my spiritual path, I know all my needs will be met. I thrive on the faith that life doesn't always have to make sense at a given moment. I can surrender all concerns to my benevolent Source. These are *my* positive core beliefs.

Since we make it all up, we can rearrange our lives to be spectacular expressions of our favorite dreams! As we make room for bigger and brighter realities, it all becomes possible.

Since our lives reflect our belief systems, why not believe life is a fantastic, creative, joyous, and fulfilling journey teaming with prosperity and synchronicity? And while we're at it, let's believe that it doesn't have to take super-human effort.

---

[2] Cindy White, *Pregnancy After 50: Redefining Family and Achieving Parenthood* (coming in 2025 from Game Shift Press)

Believe in a life where wonderful people surround you, and you're satisfied no matter what comes your way. A powerful self-fulfilling prophecy like this is as good as it gets.

You now know that everything serves your highest good, even unpleasant and confusing situations. Our challenges are for our benefit. We get to shift our perspective and discover the treasures locked away in each moment.

Life is like an artist's canvas that presents a painting in washable paint. If you don't like what you see, pull out your moistened rag, scrub away what you don't like, and paint your life into your favorite new picture!

Weave your life into a tapestry of creativity and joy without faulty concepts. Sculpt your visions. Paint your life big and beautiful, vivid, and deep, knowing that you cannot get it wrong. Sing, dance, and celebrate in your own unique way. Use your talents to make your life an amazing, happy journey.

Our life is really like that. It is meant to be a playground of imaginative fun and endless discovery. Push beyond the limits of who you think you are and what you think you can become, because that's where your best self lies. Dare to make big life changes.

Discard your self-judgments and worries about what others might think of you; none of that is real anyway. Allow others to be whoever they are. Being Ok with others, you'll detach yourself from the influence of their concepts. You will become totally at peace with yourself.

Take the time to learn new things. Never stop educating yourself. This is the final frontier of breaking free from the prison of crazy concepts! Empty that cup and be thirsty for knowledge.

Everyone has fears, doubts, rampant concepts, and an always-present ego barking at them. Knowing this, you can forgive others for their heartbreaking shortcomings, even when they bleed their nonsense into your world. As you forgive, you have compassion. You can see through their story and bring your love where it is badly needed.

Instead of needing approval from the insane, you are an example of liberation, and you are content with yourself and your choices. You are grounded and sensible amidst the craziness; you offer balance in an unbalanced world and comfort in your perfection-free lifestyle.

You are darling, adorable, sincere, and unique! Your life now has the space to become who you would most like to be.

Hopefully, your awareness of your capacity will be much larger having read this book. I hope, as you look around, you will see that nothing has changed, and yet everything has.

Deepening into the ever-promising present moment in meditation sounds a bit more inviting. Waking up from ego-based concepts opens the view to so much more.

I wish you nothing short of a miraculous life that flows from your new, fresh, and thriving choices, all made possible because of a beautiful set of new eyes.

Special Thanks ...

... go to the following people who brought their intelligence and unique angles to this book, finessing it into a better expression.

Julie Thomas, my chief editor extraordinaire.

My dear girlfriend, Sheri Leigh, who can always beat me at scrabble.

My wonderful dad, David White, who offered many edits at the age of 87, still bright, clear, and great with the English language.

Deborah Nelson, my cover producer, original author and publication teacher, and great girlfriend.

You are all treasures. I'm so very touched by the gift of your contributions.

~ Cindy White

Publications

- Byron Katie with Stephen Michell, *Loving What Is, Revised Edition: Four Questions That Can Change Your Life; The Revolutionary Process Called "The Work,"* 2021. Harmony; revised edition.

- Marci Shimoff & Carol Kline, *Happy for No Reason: 7 Steps to Being Happy from the Inside Out,* 2008. Free Press.

- Susan Jeffers, *Feel the Fear and Do It Anyway*, 2006. 20th Anniversary edition, Ballantine Books.

- Helen Schucman, William Thetford, Kenneth Wapnik (Eds.), *A Course in Miracles, Combined Volume, Third Edition*, 2007. Foundation for Inner Peace.

- T. Harv Eker, *Secrets of the Millionaire Mind,* 2005. Harper Business.

- Eckhart Tolle, *The Power of Now*, 2004. New World Library.

- Don Miguel Ruiz, *The Four Agreements*, 1997. Amber-Allen Publishing.

- Paul Selig, *I Am the Word*: A Guide to the Consciousness of Man's Self in a Transitioning Time, 2014. Gildan Media LLC.

- Machaelle Small Wright, *Behaving as if the God in All Life Mattered, Third Revised Edition*, 1997. Perelandra.

- Alan Watts, *The Book: On the Taboo Against Knowing Who You Are*, 1989. Vintage Books.

Cindy White's Publications

- Cindy M. White, *You Get There by BEING THERE: Spiritual Quotes,* 2010. Game Shift Press.

- Cindy M. White, *101 Answers to my Beloved; The Necessary Questions to Create Happily Ever After,* 2011. Game Shift Press.

- Cindy M. White, *The Ripple Effect Game for Personal and Planetary Transformation, First Edition,* 2012. Game Shift Press.

- Cindy M. White, *Crazy Useless Concepts and Breaking Through Them,* 2025. Game Shift Press.

Upcoming Publications

- Cindy M. White, *Pregnancy After 50: Redefining Family and Achieving Parenthood* (coming in 2025 from Game Shift Press).

- Cindy M. White, *Sadhu* (coming in 2025 from Game Shift Press).

- Cindy M. White, *The Awareness Eating Plan; Addiction Free, Toxin Free, Guilt Free Consumption* (coming in 2026 from Game Shift Press).

www.ingramcontent.com/pod-product-compliance
Lightning Source LLC
Chambersburg PA
CBHW072351090426
42741CB00012B/3009